DATE DUE	

The Thrift Debacle

The Thrift Debacle

Ned Eichler

UNIVERSITY OF CALIFORNIA PRESS
BERKELEY LOS ANGELES LONDON

University of California Press
Berkeley and Los Angeles, California

University of California Press, Ltd.
London, England

©1989 by
The Regents of the University of California

Printed in the United States of America
1   2   3   4   5   6   7   8   9

Library of Congress Cataloging-in-Publication Data

Eichler, Ned.
    The thrift debacle / Ned Eichler.
        p.   cm.
    Bibliography: p.
    Includes index.
    ISBN 0-520-06631-6 (alk. paper)
    1. Building and loan associations—United States—History—20th
century.   2. Savings-banks—United States—History—20th century.
3. Board of Governors of the Federal Reserve Bank (U.S.)—History.
4. Banks and banking—United States—State supervision—History—
20th century.   I. Title.
HG2151.E34   1989
332.3'2'09730904—dc20   88-40554
                                                            CIP

Contents

Preface

By the time this book is published, a new president and a new Congress will have taken office. Together they will cope with the aftermath of the greatest regulatory fiasco in American history—the obligations of the Federal Savings and Loan Insurance Corporation (FSLIC) to thrift depositors. When, for the first time, federal deposit insurance was provided by the Federal Deposit Insurance Corporation (FDIC) for commercial and savings banks in 1933 and for savings and loan associations in 1934, the programs' sponsors did not realize what they had wrought. They knew, however, that after three American depressions and several major recessions over the preceding 150 years, during which banks had failed in ever-greater numbers and with ever-greater losses, something had to be done.

Savings and loans, whose principal function was financing home construction and purchase, had never before been federally regulated. They had experienced significant losses only after 1929. Had they not been given deposit insurance, their substantial contribution to residential mortgage lending would have ended. But New Dealers were desperate to prop up the collapsing mortgage market and to promote home construction. Thus, in a fateful decision, they decided both to insure savings and loans' deposits and to do so through FSLIC, an agency separate from FDIC, the banks' insurer.

For the next forty years all went well, but then changing circumstances began to undermine the foundations of the thrift industry. Simultaneously, government deregulation came into vogue. Lifting the regulatory shackles from savings and loans came to be seen as a solution to all their problems. Those few industry leaders and analysts who warned that a bad situation would only be made worse by deregulation were overwhelmed by its proponents. Government administrators, members of Congress, and trade association officials, all usually careful policymakers, ignored basic realities and tossed prudence overboard. However inapplicable deregulation was to thrifts and whatever dangers it threatened, the approach's appeal overcame reason. In the end, it was not venality or evil intentions that produced losses approaching, if not exceeding, $100 billion, most of which will fall on taxpayers; rather, it was the power of an idea.

Thrift deregulation was never reconciled to seven crucial facts. First, more than enough commercial banks were already in existence. Second, the only justification for thrifts was their taking deposits and making home loans. Third, the relative and perhaps even absolute need for them to perform this function was shrinking. Fourth, primarily because of deposit insurance but also because of tax benefits and regulatory advantages not given to banks, thrifts were creatures of the federal government. Fifth, thrift capital was virtually nonexistent by 1980. Sixth, undercapitalized American financial institutions had a long history of making imprudent investments and going broke. And seventh, the losses could be enormous and would belong to the taxpayer.

Full deregulation required giving up the protection of depository institutions enacted in the 1930s and enhanced thereafter. In other words, it meant abandoning deposit insurance. If all restrictions had been removed, there would have been a bloody war among the 15,000 banks and 4,600 savings and loans that existed in 1980, the duration and consequences of which could not be known. No deregulation zealot addressed the contradictions. Instead, members of Congress were told that somehow deposit insurance, the special role of thrifts, and deregulation could coexist with only positive results. Delighted to avoid the unpleasant implications—that is, that not just the number but also the assets of thrifts had to be reduced—Congress bought a gigantic pig in a poke. Ideological puritans in the Reagan administration went wild. Together they produced the thrift debacle.

1

The Golden Years and the Great Depression

The Economy and the Nation

Supported by the programs enacted in 1933 and 1934, thrifts entered their heyday during the period of America's stunning economic growth after World War II. In the previous long-wave business cycle, from 1897 to 1932, savings and loan associations, like virtually all economic institutions, had operated for the last time with minimal aid from or control by the government. The Progressive Movement had led to some state and federal regulation, notably of railroads and monopolies, but the impact on the economy was minor. The Federal Reserve System, created in 1913 to stabilize and regulate commercial banks, had more effect but did not seriously inhibit the conduct of private business activity. Even World War I had little disruptive effect on the economy; in fact, insofar as it stimulated exports, the war was beneficial.

Since price stability (slight deflation) and rapid growth of the gross national product (GNP) prevailed after the 1920–1921 recession, with only two gentle downturns in 1924 and 1927, almost everyone came to believe in the perpetual benefits of American capitalism. Economists who had studied business cycles for years concluded that depressions and even serious recessions could recur only as a consequence of an external shock, such as a war or natural disaster. When the Great Depression of 1929–1932 struck, they advanced various explanations. However, subsequent economic intervention by the federal government stemmed not from revised economic theory but from political reality. Those elected in 1932 could not just tell their constituents to endure the pain. Without corrective government action, they feared, capitalism itself was doomed. Capitalist governments, including that of the United States, were about to assume a new responsibility—putting a floor under GNP and a ceiling on unemployment and guaranteeing a minimum standard of living. This was the meaning of the New Deal.

Banks

Despite acts establishing the National Banking System in 1863 and the Federal Reserve System fifty years later, the number and assets of banks continued to rise exponentially. The new legislation was only minimally effective for the same two reasons that Andrew Jackson's attempted restrictions on banking had been unsuccessful in the 1830s. First, economic growth and free enterprise were considered sacrosanct, and the role of government was to support, not restrain, them. People immigrated to the United States to escape feudal and mercantile restrictions. Calvin Coolidge was on the mark in contending that "the business of America is business." Second, the nation was founded and settled in opposition to central authority's encroachment on not only economic but also civil liberty. The principal American defenses against this threat were the separation of powers within the national government, the Bill of Rights, and the primacy of the states. The last in particular had tied Jackson's hands; one result was free banking. Like Jackson, the U.S. Comptroller of the Currency, who was the federal regulator under the National Banking Act, faced a resurgence of state banks established to escape his dominion, though he often moderated restrictive regulations of national banks after 1863. States' rights likewise limited the effectiveness of the Federal Reserve.

The states competed with federal agencies through lenience, allowing lower capital ratios and greater freedom in lending, for example, especially on real estate. They also permitted pyramiding, under which small, mostly rural banks could count deposits in money center banks as reserves. The Federal Reserve System, which requires member banks to hold their reserves in Federal Reserve banks rather than in private correspondents, tried to eliminate this practice. Its success was limited. The states impeded its effort by restricting or even prohibiting the establishment of branch offices, thereby ensuring the continued existence of a large number of small banks. The owners and managers of these banks opposed branching because it was a means by which larger institutions could destroy them. Thus, the pattern that had begun to take shape in the 1830s was politically self-fulfilling. The federal government could not override the states, which had become the political captives of the small banks under their jurisdiction. Large banks found a way to play the two levels of jurisdiction against each other, a game that would have dire consequences in the 1980s.

In 1900 there were over 12,000 commercial banks, with over $9 billion in assets. The peak number of banks in American history, 30,000, was reached in 1922, and total assets climbed steadily to $52 billion, more than five times the amount at the turn of the century. Although state-chartered nonmember banks accounted for most of the decline in number after 1922—the number fell by nearly 6,000 in the next seven years—in 1929 there were still over 13,000, with 25 percent of total bank assets. Whereas there were fewer than 1,200 state-chartered member banks, their total assets, which grew faster, were slightly higher. Thus, sixty-six years after the creation of the National Banking System and sixteen years after the creation of the Federal Reserve System, despite continued relaxation of regulations to meet state competition, only about 43 percent of all commercial banks, with less than 50 percent of total assets, had come under the full jurisdiction of the federal government. Those who had dreamed of a unified, strictly regulated banking system, which would provide American capitalism with the services it required and at the same time contribute to stability, had been disappointed.

Well before the stock market crash of 1929, the banking system had shown its vulnerability. Lending on stocks was a comparatively new practice, the danger of which was demonstrated when the crash came. But two other forms of security, agricultural land and products and urban real estate, which had given banks trouble in the five or ten years before previous depressions, did so again in the 1920s. As in the decade before the depression of 1893–1896, so too from 1922 to 1929 a segment of agriculture did poorly even as the rest of the economy did well. Once more the world capacity to raise certain farm products had outstripped demand. The results were sharp price declines and many bankruptcies. Annual housing starts peaked at 937,000 units in 1925 and fell consistently thereafter. As in agriculture, there were pockets of far more severe market deterioration, Florida for example, where a speculative real estate boom broke in 1926.

As in the past, banks, mainly small ones outside major metropolitan areas, were caught with loans on assets whose value had fallen sharply. From 1922 to 1929, 5,712 banks, with $1.6 billion in assets, failed. This constituted 20.3 percent of the number of banks but only 3.8 percent of the deposits. State nonmember banks, mostly small ones, accounted for a disproportionate number of the failures, over 75 percent, and 65 percent of the assets. State member institutions, the largest banks, were hardly affected at all. A contemporary observer, Professor Charles S. Tippetts, gave the following bleak depiction: "The past eight years constitute one of the darkest chapters in all American banking history. . . . One of the chief explanations for this disgraceful debacle may be found in the structure of our dual banking system. It is impossible to create a unified banking system of high standards and sound banking practices as long as each state tries to build up its own banking system at the expense of the national banks."[1] State-federal duality was not the only form of regulatory competition, however. With the creation of the Federal Reserve System a struggle emerged between it and the Comptroller of the Currency, the regulator designated under the National Banking System.

What was first believed to be an isolated event, the stock market's precipitous fall in 1929, was followed by a general economic downturn. When the latter became not just a recession, as in 1920–1921, but a major depression that dwarfed its predecessors, the banking system's problems mounted. Over 5,000 more banks, with $3.2 billion in assets, failed from 1930 to 1932. Although the number of failures was slightly smaller than it had been over the previous eight years, the assets involved were double the earlier amount. State nonmember banks still accounted disproportionately for both the number and assets of failed institutions, but during the Depression even some large member banks were clearly in trouble. When Roosevelt took office, he feared that only drastic action could forestall total disaster.

Thrifts

The clear distinction between thrifts—savings and loans and savings banks—and commercial banks was blurred after the creation of the Federal Reserve System. The former held only time (savings) deposits, which paid interest and could not be withdrawn except at the end of specified periods. Commercial banks held mostly demand (increasingly checking) accounts, which generally did not bear interest after 1913, although that had been an earlier practice. Because funds deposited in commercial banks were largely on call, investments were supposed to be short-term. However, banks often strayed from this doctrine. After 1913 restrictions against commercial banks' taking of time deposits were relaxed, allowing them to compete more vigorously for savings.

Although savings and loans and savings banks performed similar depository functions, dissimilarities pertained until well into this century. There was some reduction in differences after 1900, and considerably more after 1945. By 1980 both types of thrifts operated identically. Yet the organizing impulse of each was different: savings banks were established to promote careful money management, savings and loans to foster home ownership. Until after the Civil War, savings banks were prohibited from or restricted in lending on real estate. Not until the early 1900s did mortgages approach 50 percent of their total investments. In contrast, mortgages were virtually the only investment for savings and loans, except during wartime. Furthermore, savings banks made a significant percentage of their real estate loans on properties other than individual homes, as much as 40 percent, while savings and loans were almost exclusively lenders on owner-occupied houses.

In 1929 there were 11,777 savings and loans and 592 savings banks. The average size of the former was $1.3 million; of the latter, $18.9 million. From 1930 on, the number of both types of institution fell consistently, though at a steeper rate for savings and loans. By 1940 there were only 7,521 savings and loans, a 40 percent decline, whereas the decline of savings banks was less than 10 percent, to 540. Despite the Depression, total assets in savings banks rose by almost 15 percent in the decade. Savings and loans fared far less well, with total assets at $5.7 billion in 1940, almost 40 percent below the 1929 level.

Savings and loans were far more dependent on the

production of single-family residences and the number of owners seeking mortgages than any other type of lender. By 1930 almost half of American families owned their homes. The percentage of owners with mortgages rose from 31.7 in 1900 to 45.3 in 1940. After housing starts rose from 204,000 in 1900 to 405,000 in 1919, they fell again, to 247,000 in 1920. Following the 1920–1921 recession, the rate rose dramatically for four years, to a peak of 937,000 units in 1925, but then fell steadily, to 509,000 in 1929 and reaching the nadir of 93,000 in 1933. This rapid increase in home production was the underlying cause of savings and loan growth after the turn of the century. It also aided savings banks, but to a lesser degree. By the same token, when starts dwindled almost to nothing and foreclosures skyrocketed after 1929, savings and loans suffered the most.

When restrictions on taking savings accounts were relaxed, commercial banks quickly came to dominate the field. By 1920 they had 61.1 percent of all the country's savings, compared to 27.8 percent for savings banks and 10 percent for savings and loans. This predominance lasted until after World War II. However, for reasons already cited, by 1930 savings and loans were already the nation's leading holders of all residential mortgages, at 37.8 percent, compared to 17.5 percent for commercial banks and 27.0 percent for savings banks.

As demonstrated in the depression of 1893–1896 and again in the Great Depression, commercial banks were at greater risk than thrifts because of their high proportion of demand deposits, especially since their capital ratios had consistently fallen and since they had strayed so far from making only safe, short-term loans. Whereas thrifts, whose real estate loans had a longer term and higher interest rate, appeared to be at greater risk, most commercial bank real estate loans were secured by farms or homes in rural areas, where values fell sharply even in the 1920s, not to mention the 1930s. Among thrifts, savings banks had substantially higher reserves than savings and loans; they had shorter-term loans—generally five years versus ten—lower interest rates, and lower loan-to-value ratios. For these reasons, they got through the Depression less scathed than either commercial banks or fellow thrifts. Ironically, although savings and loans did experience severe problems with real estate loans during the Depression, their greatest source of losses was from their deposits in commercial banks.

Not only did the number of housing starts tumble; so did real estate values, a drop of even greater importance to thrifts. Many people who lost jobs and wealth were unable to make mortgage or rent payments; when lenders foreclosed and put property up for sale, they were only adding to a glutted market. Herbert Hoover, who had a special interest in thrifts, moved in 1932 to provide relief to institutions and home owners through two new agencies, the Reconstruction Finance Corporation (RFC) and the Federal Home Loan Bank System—but his response was already late. From 1929 through 1932, 597 savings and loans, with $411 million in assets, had failed. The number of foreclosures had soared from a pre-Depression average of 73,000 per year to 273,000 in 1932.

Both the Reconstruction Finance Corporation and the Federal Home Loan banks provided liquidity to thrifts, about $275 million. Of far greater significance was the Home Owners Loan Corporation (HOLC), created in

1933. HOLC propped up the housing market for the rest of the decade, refinancing three-quarters of a billion dollars of home mortgages—on more than a million homes—formerly held by private lenders. Its advances totaled $3.1 billion, including the purchase of $525 million in mortgages from commercial banks, $410 million in mortgages from savings banks, and $770 million in mortgages from savings and loans.

These federal capital infusions, together with a modest but steady economic recovery from 1933 to 1937, allowed savings banks to survive almost intact and savings and loans to avert a complete disaster. Nevertheless, during the whole decade of the 1930s, a total of 1,706 associations failed, with losses to depositors of about $200 million. Most thrifts, along with other mortgage lenders, behaved as they had after the 1893–1896 depression. They took title to foreclosed property and, instead of selling it immediately, reconditioned it, paid the taxes, and rented it. On average, home values had fallen 40 percent, an amount just about equal to the equity behind savings and loan mortgages (savings bank loan-to-value ratios were lower; the equity was therefore higher). When the costs of foreclosure, refurbishing, lost interest, and the like were added to the mortgages, the total was usually higher than the immediate sale value. By holding on to the below-market-value mortgages and riding the gradual inflation that began in 1933, most thrifts were able to avoid severe losses. Savings and loans' total foreclosures amounted to $5 billion. The value of real estate owned (taken by foreclosure) rose from $238 million in 1930 to a peak of $1.2 billion in 1936. Even in 1941 it was still more than double the 1930 level.

Government Reform

Funding from Federal Home Loan banks, RFC, and HOLC staved off a complete savings and loan disaster. So did Federal Reserve bank advances to commercial banks and the reversal of federal monetary policy, when the money supply was again loosened after the initial tightening from 1929 to 1931. Roosevelt went further, closing all banks, a bitterly disputed decision. However effective these actions were, officialdom still searched for fundamental ways to prevent recurrent financial collapses, which, if they did not cause the fall in production and rise in unemployment, exacerbated it. Three new mechanisms—federal chartering, deposit insurance, and Federal Housing Administration (FHA) mortgage insurance—eventually changed the environment for banking, especially for savings and loans, and for housing finance. Those who created these mechanisms could not accurately predict their consequences. Nevertheless, they did sense what the future has shown clearly—the American public's absolute aversion to financial disasters and depressions.

The original purpose of the Home Loan Bank System was to provide liquidity to savings and loans. The next year, as the Roosevelt administration began trying out a number of ways to improve the economy, the system was assigned a second function: to seek members, which would then be subject to federal rather than state control. This same purpose had underlain the creation of the National Banking System, which had offered banks "bribes," such as exemption from a tax on note issues, in return for their subjecting themselves to restrictions tighter than those applied by the states. The Home Loan

Bank Board's offer of a $100,000 government deposit proved, however, to be an insufficient inducement to most thrift managers. Since, in addition, only mutual companies could get a federal charter, membership in the new system grew slowly. In 1935 only 8 percent of all savings and loans had joined. By 1960 membership included just 28 percent.

Of far greater importance than the Bank Board System was insurance for deposits through the Federal Savings and Loan Insurance Corporation (FSLIC), created in 1934. A year earlier, a sister agency, the Federal Deposit Insurance Corporation (FDIC), had been set up to insure bank deposits. Most savings banks, those that had the required reserves, chose FDIC. Yet savings and loans, even those that might have qualified for FDIC membership, joined FSLIC for one overriding reason: they felt more comfortable with an agency established solely to serve them. They knew insurance would involve costs and regulations. The latter, they thought, could best be mitigated if the regulator was not beholden to thrifts' main competitors, the far more numerous and richer commercial banks. The industry's trade association, the U.S. League for Savings Associations, had been in existence since 1892, but the necessity to lobby the new federal agencies greatly enhanced its role. The League immediately proved its worth when it gained reduction of the insurance premium from 0.25 percent to 0.125 percent. From then to the present, the League has had as much, if not more, influence over savings and loan legislation and regulations than any other trade association. Thrifts could join FSLIC while remaining under state jurisdiction, a replication of the commercial bank arrangement. As with the Home Loan

Bank System, membership growth was slow. By 1935 only 12.1 percent of all institutions had joined. Ultimately, however, most savings and loans found insurance essential in attracting deposits, and by 1960 the membership percentage had climbed to 94.3.

State deposit insurance for banks had existed well before 1933, in fact even before the Civil War. New York set up a safety fund first, in 1829; it was followed by Indiana, Iowa, Michigan, Ohio, and Vermont. Only the last was unable to pay all depositor losses. While such systems were theoretically made superfluous by the National Banking System, eight states set up new forms of insurance after the resurgence of state banking in the 1880s and the panics of 1893 and 1907. Support came largely from country bankers. In 1923 the agricultural price decline crippled deposit insurance in the affected regions. By 1929, even before the Great Depression began, all the state systems had been wiped out, leaving depositors with substantial losses.

The Federal Housing Administration was created in 1935, principally to promote home production by making financing more attractive. By charging a premium and providing insurance, it induced private lenders to reduce down payments and extend the length of loans. FHA's impact until 1945 was minor, but after the war it contributed mightily to making effective the demand for new housing, which in the previous decade and a half had been pent up by low production rates. Down payments, formerly 40 percent of the amount of the loan, soon became as low as 3 percent, and loan terms, which had been ten to twelve years at most, were stretched out to thirty-five or even forty years. In addition to fulfilling its primary purpose, that of facilitating home production, FHA mortgage insurance was used extensively for postwar apartment development. FHA also insured construction loans, thereby immensely aiding undercapitalized builders. Savings banks became major FHA lenders; savings and loans did not. However, FHA had an effect far beyond the actual mortgages insured. Prior to its existence, mortgage terms, documents, and conditions were highly localized. They could not easily be sold or even hypothecated. FHA demonstrated the safety of long-term, low-down-payment loans and, through standardization, made them marketable throughout the country. This was the sine qua non for the ultimate establishment of a secondary market, in which mortgages could become fungible.

Conclusion

From 1932 to 1935, in reaction to the financial and economic failures of the Great Depression, the basic federal rules under which thrifts and banks were to operate for the next forty-five years were put into place. They added to conflict not only between the states and the national government but also among federal agencies. Who was to decide minimum net worth and reserves, portfolio composition, underwriting standards, geographic limits on lending and deposit taking—the Comptroller of the Currency, the Federal Reserve Board, the Home Loan Bank Board, FDIC, FSLIC, or state authorities? The frequent duplication of state agencies, with one agency for banks and another for thrifts, further complicated the conflict.

During the unprecedented period of prosperity and stability from shortly after World War II until 1966, regulatory competition seemed healthy. As inflation mounted, as credit crunches became more frequent and more serious, and as new methods for taking in savings and providing credit emerged, the regulatory structure of depository institutions in general and thrifts in particular came under fire. A series of recommendations poured out from reform commissions. Yet the system existing in 1935 remained essentially intact until 1980. By then, many, including a host of intellectuals, were demanding not merely a moratorium but also a rollback of the government intervention that had pervaded all capitalist economies in the preceding forty-five years. Counterrevolution was in the air and would have its day.

2

The Keynesian Miracle: 1945–1966

The Economy

Despite all the initiatives of the New Deal, or, as some contend, because of the atmosphere it engendered, the American economic recovery after 1932 was slow and intermittent. When war began in Europe in 1939, GNP had barely regained the 1929 level and unemployment was still stubbornly at a high 14 percent. Supplying the Allies provided a stimulant, but at the end of 1941 unemployment remained at over 10 percent. Many economists, recognizing that the United States resumed rapid economic growth only after its direct entry into the war, feared that peace would throw the country back into depression or, at best, return it to the pace of the late 1930s.

This bleak prognosis was wildly off the mark, though, for in the twenty-five years from 1948 to 1973 economic growth was rapid in the United States, as in virtually all developed or semideveloped nations of the world. Rather than declining, the rate of growth of per capita GNP rose to 2.2 percent per year, compared to the 1.8 percent rate that had prevailed from the Civil War to 1940. Impressive as this increase was, growth was higher in the same period in every other developed, noncommunist nation. Indeed, in Italy, Germany, Japan, and Austria it was more than twice as high. Even England surpassed the United States, though not by much.

A number of factors contributed to the postwar economic boom, the following among them:

1. Low levels of production during the 1930s and the war years had built up substantial demand.
2. The war had destroyed or damaged facilities, many of which were obsolete. Grim though its costs were in human life and suffering, the war was in part a giant program of economically useful demolition.
3. The war had broken down many of the barriers restricting the mobility of labor and capital. It had also led to the introduction and development of new technology applicable in peacetime.
4. The rate of population growth, instead of continuing to decline as it had done since the 1920s, surged upward.
5. The government institutionalized a high rate of spending. Government spending in the United States went from about 10 percent of GNP in 1929 to 33 percent, and in some European countries to 50 percent or more, ensuring an important and brand-new underpinning for demand.
6. Existing technology such as electronics had yet to be substantially exploited, and basic research in a number of areas suggested that useful technology was about to be developed. There were plenty of opportunities for innovating entrepreneurs to

seize. This was also true of new financial forms, e.g., the fully amortized home mortgage. As a result of alterations in ownership structure, e.g., larger farms, and technology, improvement in agricultural productivity increased dramatically.

The unprecedented level of economic growth in the United States and in other capitalist countries was not the only product of these factors. Equally surprising was the degree of economic stability that ensued. From 1948 to 1973 there were no sharp recessions, let alone a depression. Almost universally, economists concluded that cyclicity was no longer a serious problem and turned their attention to other matters such as income distribution and productivity. Many took up econometrics, because of the wealth of material made available by improved communications, the proliferation of information-gathering departments of government, and the availability of computers to sort and collate the data.

No one claimed that all cyclical variations had been eliminated; in fact, there were three mild recessions during the Eisenhower years. John Kennedy therefore began to accept a thesis propounded by many economists: by cutting taxes, government could so stimulate economic growth that tax revenues would more than offset the initial tax rate reduction. The proponents of this idea, now called supply-siders, were taking Keynesianism further than Keynes himself had. They believed that Eisenhower's fiscal policies had been too timid and that the Federal Reserve Board (the Fed) under William McChesney Martin had restrained the money supply too much. The cornerstone of Kennedy's attempt at economic stimulation was a tax credit for capital investment. Lyndon Johnson pushed the idea further and, in many people's view, corrupted it. As spending for the Vietnam War increased, he neither raised taxes substantially nor reduced domestic spending but drove his Great Society program through the Congress. The result was an acceleration of the inflation rate to double digits in the 1970s from the creeping 1 to 2 percent that had prevailed from about 1950 until 1966.

The Housing Market

Housing production in the United States, like the economy as a whole, has followed a cyclical pattern. Housing starts mounted from the mid-1870s, began to decline in 1890, and rebounded just before 1900. After the interruption of World War I, they continued to rise, peaking in 1925. The low construction levels that lasted from 1925 through World War II, combined with a reversal of the low rates of population growth that had prevailed in the 1920s and 1930s and postwar demobilization, laid the basis for a residential construction boom. Yet if masses of people wanting improved housing were the only requirement for generating production, construction would soar in countries like China and India. Need establishes potential, which can be realized only when demand is made effective. In European countries devastated by war, this was accomplished largely by direct government action, whereas in the United States the instrument was primarily private builders of suburban homes and apartment buildings. These entrepreneurs, however, could not have performed their miracles without a supportive climate at every level of government and the burgeoning economic growth that was both a crucial precondition for and a result of the rise in housing production.

I have described the postwar setting for home building elsewhere.[1] Briefly, it consisted of the following:

1. An abundant inventory of land at the edges of existing settlements
2. A major government effort, financed largely at the federal level, to build a national network of highways connecting metropolitan areas and providing access from outlying undeveloped land to city jobs
3. Inexpensive fuel for cars
4. State and local governments willing and even anxious to provide the infrastructure required for housing construction—water lines, sewers, roads, schools, and so forth—and to grant necessary zoning and building permits
5. Mortgage financing that allowed undercapitalized builders to produce, and young families to purchase, homes

While private lenders supplied the loans, they could not have done so without federal aid in the form of deposit insurance, FHA insurance, and Veterans Administration (VA) guarantees (similar to FHA insurance but with even lower down payments) or in the absence of two regulatory provisions for banks and thrifts. First, under Regulation Q, the Fed limited the interest rate banks could pay on time deposits, thus allowing thrifts to outbid banks for savings deposits. Second, as a quid pro quo, savings and loans were required to invest the great majority of those funds in home loans in exchange for being given favorable income tax treatment. Had banks, whose main business was commercial lending, been able to compete equally for savings or had thrifts been free to make non–real estate loans, less money would have been available for housing.

Thrifts

Thrift deposits and assets mounted after the war. However, the return on those assets and on net worth rose only until 1955; it then began to fall. Ultimately this decline in profits spurred deregulation. In addition, savings and loans came to be the dominant type of thrift. Their growth was unprecedented. In 1945 there were 6,149 associations, less than half the number in 1925, 12,403. Yet assets had risen from $5.5 billion to $8.7 billion over those same twenty years. Twenty years later, in 1965, the number of firms was virtually unchanged, but assets had grown to $110.4 billion, over twelve times the 1945 level.

Clearly, savings and loans grew along with the population, the economy, and especially the housing market. But their rate of growth was even faster than other lenders' as they raised their market share. In 1945 they held about 35 percent of the country's home loans; by 1965 they had almost half. Although the proportion held by savings banks fell slightly, the main losers were commercial banks and life insurance companies.

FHA had little impact on mortgage lending until after the war, when virtually all thrift home loans were still conventional. In 1955, however, 44 percent of the mortgages made by savings and loans were VA or FHA, and for savings banks the percentage was even higher. As the postwar era progressed, the thrifts' percentage of conventional loans increased. They continued to concentrate on home lending but gradually increased the share of apartment loans in their portfolios.

Savings and loans had made a small portion of their loans for new construction before the Depression. In the late 1930s, as home building rose and lenders sought outlets for funds, construction lending increased dramatically, reaching 30 percent or more of all savings and loan lending. After dropping in 1945, construction lending again rose, as indicated by the course of origination fees, which are higher on construction than on permanent loans. In 1945 fee income for savings and loans was 2.5 percent of total income, rising to 7.4 percent in 1955 and to 8.5 percent in 1960, the peak year. By 1965, however, fee income had fallen to 4.3 percent.

Thrift lending activity, including that of savings banks, followed the cycle of residential construction and home sales, both of which tended to lead the economy into and then out of recessions. In addition, since interest rates usually rose in the latter part of a recovery and did not start to decline until the country was well into a recession, the cost of funds increased for thrifts while business was receding. Savings and loans' gross and net income fluctuated accordingly.

There are several ways to look at income and expense. One measurement is percentage of total assets: for savings and loans the return on assets rose steadily to a high of 1 percent in 1961 and then declined until the 1970s; it was down to 0.65 percent in 1965. Another measurement is return on net worth, which apparently peaked at 12.7 percent in 1960 and also went down thereafter, falling to 9.7 percent in 1965. For savings banks the high point for the return on assets, 1.38 percent, came much earlier, in 1945; by 1960 it had fallen to 0.36 percent. This inferior profit performance was not caused by high savings bank expenses, which rose only slightly, from 0.65 percent of assets in 1945 to 0.69 percent in 1960. The savings and loan expense ratio was almost double that of savings banks, although instead of rising it fell slightly, from 1.34 percent in 1950 to 1.21 percent in 1960. As a share of income, however, expenses fell dramatically for savings and loans, from 27 percent in 1950 to 19 percent in 1965.

Despite the improvement in relative operating costs and despite continued growth, returns on assets and net worth declined for savings and loans after 1955. Their main competitors for savings were commercial banks, whose interest rates on deposits were set by the Fed under Regulation Q. Thrifts, which were not so restricted, paid between 50 and 100 basis points more than banks to attract the deposits needed to make the loans that generated the growth in assets. They were unable to gain increases in loan rates equivalent to the increases paid for their savings. Furthermore, their deposits were short-term, while their loans were fixed in rate for twenty-five or more years. As inflation gradually rose in the early 1960s, the spread between interest cost and interest collected narrowed. Higher origination volume, lower relative operating costs, and increased fees from construction lending helped but were insufficient to offset the negative drag of narrowing margins. What was a mild difficulty in the early 1960s, however, became a crisis fifteen years later when inflation was running rampant.

Savings and loans differed substantially by type of charter and by location. Federally chartered associations—all mutuals—were less than one-third the total number and held over half the assets. One-third of the state-chartered institutions were not FSLIC-insured (some participated in state insurance programs), but they had less than 10 percent of the assets of state associations. Whereas only one-sixth (768) of the state associations were stock companies, they had about one-quarter of the assets and, moreover, were concentrated in four states: Illinois, Texas, Ohio, and California.

California—A Special Case

With $521 million, or 6 percent of assets of all associations in 1945, California savings and loans were a modest presence on the national scene. Over the next twenty years, however, the state's institutions became a unique and dominant force. By 1965 assets had grown to $27.3 billion, 20 percent of the nation's total. Even more impressive was the difference in association size. In California average assets had risen to almost $100 million, compared to $20 million for the nation as a whole. When savings and loans within the state are disaggregated, an even more dramatic picture appears. For example, while stock companies represented 25 percent of associations for the nation as a whole, the percentage was 65 in California. Large and small companies differed tremendously too. The top ten, with assets of $300 million or more, had 44 percent of total assets; the three largest firms—American, Home, and Great Western—had 30 percent of the total. Home and American had already emerged as mammoth institutions, each with over $2 billion in assets. Neither in California nor anywhere else had any other association acquired even $1 billion.

The exponential growth of California savings and loans occurred disproportionately in the southern part of the state, where nine of the ten largest associations were based. But associations in California and especially in southern California were unusual in ways other than size. In almost every operational aspect, California associations functioned differently from those elsewhere. One underlying reason, of course, was the scale of the state's housing production, about 20 percent of the nation's total, coupled with the shortage of savings to provide the necessary mortgage funds. Savings and loans thus needed to be especially aggressive in attracting local deposits and in importing money. They secured money from outside the state in two ways. First, they advertised for mail deposits, mainly in the Northeast, where a bonus of as little as 0.25 percent over the rate paid by a local association would produce a flood of funds. Second, California savings and loans, which had more lending opportunities than local depositors could meet, sold whole loans or participations to their counterparts in the East, whose position was the reverse. In 1965 California savings and loans made $3 billion in loans, of which $690 million, or almost one-fourth, were sold.

Clearly, if California institutions were paying a premium for out-of-state money, by paying directly to depositors or by selling loans to sister companies, they risked reducing profits. In fact, they found several ways to raise revenues above the increased cost. One method was simply to charge higher interest rates on permanent home loans. Another was to increase the percentages of apartment and construction lending in their portfolios, both of which generated higher yields than home loans. In 1963, the peak year, California associations made 31.5 percent of their loans on apartments and 24.1 percent on "speculative" (built for future sale) construction, percentages that far exceeded the national averages. Fees, another source of revenue, were, at about 20 percent of all income, almost double the national average.

California savings and loans competed with banks, life insurance companies, and mortgage bankers for construction and apartment financing to builders and loans to home buyers. FHA insurance and VA guarantees aided their competitors. For home buying, VA guarantees were attractive because of low interest rates and down payments. Savings and loans could and did use the FHA and VA programs, but California associations, especially those in the south, increasingly tried to avoid them for three reasons. First, although discounting was prevalent, government-imposed rate ceilings tended to limit yields. Second, both federal agencies restricted home sales prices, loan amounts, and buyer credit approval; in the case of FHA-insured construction loans, the number of starts was also restricted. These were serious problems for builders and purchasers of homes. If savings and loans could offer relief, they could increase not only overall market size but their share of it as well. Third, this liberalism in lending allowed them to charge higher interest rates and loan fees. From the late 1950s to the mid-1960s, then, California savings and loans aggressively sought to induce builders and buyers to borrow from them rather than from others and to bypass FHA and VA.

The inducements were many and varied. One was to require little or no builder equity. Another was to finance more home and apartment starts than a bank would allow. Still another was to accept types of income rejected by FHA, VA, or other lenders for credit qualification. Some managers of savings and loans invented truly ingenious devices to get business. When builders lacked the required equity to buy and develop land, for example, savings and loans got around regulations limiting loan-to-value ratios to 75 or 80 percent by purchasing the land and granting options at a nominal initial cost. In exchange for these disguised loans, the lender-owner charged fees of 5 to 10 percent and required a first right of refusal on the construction and permanent financing. Savings and loans were using a blatant ruse to frustrate the intent of federal and state regulators.

Another scheme to circumvent the rules involved the requirement that single-family mortgages be 80 to 85 percent of savings and loan portfolios. To accommodate owner-occupants of duplexes and fourplexes, buildings with two to four units were included in the "home" category. Builders and savings and loans found a way to take advantage of this exemption: first the builders persuaded local governments to zone large sites into four-unit lots so they could construct large-scale apartment projects, sometimes containing as many as 400 units (100 four-unit buildings); then the lenders made a series of individual loans on each lot, which for regulatory purposes were counted in the "single-family" basket. Extensive lending and regulatory circumvention by savings and loans contributed mightily to a California apartment-construction boom in the early 1960s. Although ordinarily two- to four-unit buildings accounted for a minuscule share of residential construction, in 1963, 14 percent of all savings and loan mortgages were made in this category.

Yet another scheme was designed to make home sales easier for builders, who wanted to offer low down payments but avoid VA or FHA restraints: by retaining title to a property and selling it on a sales contract, builders could apply their own underwriting standards. However, this could work only if the construction lender made a loan high enough to limit or even eliminate the builder's equity and extended the term of the construction loan—which is just what lenders did.

These and other practices allowed both builders and savings and loans to grow as they supplied housing to California's burgeoning population, a cooperative effort that reached its zenith in the early 1960s. The maximum annual increase in savings and loan assets, 31.3 percent, came in 1963, whereas the industry's highest return on equity, 18.6 percent, was reached a year earlier. At the same time, though, aggressive fund-raising and lending by savings and loans had ominous implications. Rapid growth and high interest rates and fees can rarely, if ever, be achieved without relaxing credit requirements. And relaxed credit increases risk. What had seemed to be an appropriate level of production soon became overbuilding and inflated values. In California a production decline began in 1963 and lasted for three years, during which time annual housing starts fell from over 300,000 to fewer than 100,000. Residential construction, especially of apartments, had simply outpaced the spectacular demand of the early 1960s. Compounding the problem was a slowdown in the state's economic and population growth. From 1963 to 1965 profit margins were halved.

In 1966 the noose on California associations tightened. Economic and population growth continued to recede, and housing production fell to a postwar low. When the Fed tried to curb inflation, interest rates rose. Of course, monetary restraint in response to heightened economic activity had adversely affected thrifts several times since 1945, but this time the situation was worse. Thrifts, especially in California, now increased deposits by bidding up the savings interest rate. But in so doing they attracted more and more "hot money," deposits that would be quickly withdrawn if better opportunities arose elsewhere. One competitive alternative to a thrift savings deposit was an account at a commercial bank; another was a Treasury bill, whose rate moves quickly. In other words, a national savings market was developing. Less able to compete for funds when interest rates rose, thrift executives stood helplessly by as money flew out the door, a process called disintermediation. From 1965 to 1966 the sale of loans by state-chartered firms fell 66 percent and "withdrawable shares" (hot money deposits) declined 25 percent.

The conditions cited above diminished both the rate of asset growth and the profit margins of California associations. The former, having fallen from its peak of 31.3 percent in 1963 to 9.7 percent in 1965, tumbled to a mere 3 percent in 1966. Returns on assets and net worth, which had fallen by one-half from 1963 to 1965, were halved again in 1966. Ominously, "scheduled items" (troubled loans) rose 50 percent from 1964 to 1965, to two and one-half times their level in 1961. The survival of a number of state savings and loans, some of them quite large, was in doubt. Several did fail, because the Home Loan Bank Board responded to the crisis too late. Largely to stop California associations from paying so much for savings and taking excessive risk, the Board imposed a national ceiling on deposit rates: to maintain the historical differential, wherein savings and loans paid more than banks, the rate was pegged at 0.25 percent above that of commercial banks.

Conclusion

The inability of California savings and loans to find lending opportunities in a depressed housing market, together with competition for savings, had already curbed their aggressive chase for deposits. The main question was, or should have been, was a significant percentage of the state's savings and loan assets subject to substantial devaluation? In other words, what was the chance of massive delinquencies and defaults causing net worth to disappear, insolvency to result, and FSLIC to incur substantial losses? In 1981 the Fed embarked on an aggressive effort to bring down the rate of inflation. It succeeded, but interest rates and inflation declined sharply only after rates had first soared and the rapid increase in real estate values had been stopped, even depressed in many instances, by a deep recession. Apparently, those advocating, crafting, and administering thrift deregulation never considered this possible course of events; the only scenario they seemed capable of imagining was continuation of the recent past—further rises in inflation, interest rates, real estate values, and GNP growth.

What might have happened to California savings and loans if the following had happened in 1966: (1) President Johnson had ended U.S. involvement in Vietnam; (2) the government had reduced its domestic spending; and (3) the Fed had decided to continue sufficient monetary restraint to make sure that inflation did not exceed the 1 percent level of the 1950s? In other words, what if the government had behaved in 1967 much as it behaved in 1981?

There would presumably have been a recession, just as there was in 1981. The last downturn before 1981 had ended in early 1975, six years earlier. If a recession had begun in 1967, the same six-year interval between recessions would have obtained. When recovery came, say in 1968, California's economic and population growth would have resumed at about its previous pace, but not higher. Real estate values would have fallen sharply and hit bottom well after the end of the recession. Virtually all the overexposed California savings and loans would have become insolvent when a high percentage of their loans went bad. Although FSLIC would have suffered severe losses satisfying depositor claims on a small number of associations, the magnitude would not have been nearly so great as in the 1980s, in part because net worth ratios were higher in the 1960s.

But of course, none of this occurred. Johnson chose to boost spending without collecting equivalent taxes to pay for it, causing the Fed to increase the money supply to fund (monetize) the resulting deficits. Instead of a recession came a government-induced boom. Instead of price stability came rising inflation. Inflation led to higher interest rates, the bane that deregulation was designed to overcome.

Ironically, the most ardent reformers of the 1980s condemned the policymakers of the late 1960s and the 1970s for lacking the discipline to avoid currency debasement, which, among its other faults, undermined thrifts. They forgot, however, or never realized in the first place, that one salutary consequence of government fiscal and monetary stimuli, whatever harm they did, was to mitigate, if not wholly prevent, losses that would otherwise have stemmed from overzealous lending. Lenders were saved by inflation not only after 1966 but twice more as well, after 1970 and 1975. After 1980, however, inflation-induced leaps in real estate values did not materialize. Thrifts and FSLIC could not escape the consequences of their improvidence. Deregulation in the 1980s was designed to fight the battles of the 1970s. The disaster that had loomed in California in the 1960s had faded from view. Even those who had seen and barely avoided it seemed to have forgotten its lesson.

3

The End of an Era:
1967–1980

The Economy

The thirty-five years from 1938 to 1973 were unique in American economic history. At no earlier time was the rate of GNP growth so rapid or so sustained. From the end of the sharp recession of 1937–1938 to the beginning of an even more serious downturn in 1973, cyclical reversals were mild. Short cycles came with regularity from the end of World War II until 1960; then came an especially long recovery, which ended in 1969 when, at least partly in response to Fed restraint, a credit crunch induced a brief recession.

Richard Nixon, elected in 1968, was acutely aware of the political fallout from economic fluctuations. He attributed his 1960 defeat to the mild recession of 1960–1961, which was caused, or at least worsened, by stringent monetary policy. Although William McChesney Martin, chairman of the Federal Reserve Board, had monetized Lyndon Johnson's deficits after 1966, thereby helping to maintain the economy's upward path, Nixon wanted his own man in the Fed. His choice was Arthur Burns, long a student of business cycles and an avowed inflation fighter. To many, the emerging menace was not slower GNP growth but rising inflation, which had reached 5 percent. The president wanted both rapid growth and price stability; he expected Burns to help him accomplish his goal. Nixon hit on a novel scheme. By imposing wage and price controls, he left the Fed free, at least temporarily, to pump the money supply, thus giving Nixon the economic environment he wanted to win reelection in 1972: high growth and low inflation.

Of course, the piper had to be paid. After winning a smashing victory, Nixon lifted controls. By 1974 inflation was over 12 percent and GNP was diving. Despite the ensuing recession and high unemployment, the Fed finally tried to curb inflation. In so doing, it exacerbated the already sharp downturn, as did an OPEC embargo and the resultant run-up in oil prices. A new word entered the economic lexicon: "stagflation." In the spring of 1975 the nation's first serious postwar recession finally hit bottom. But interest rates and inflation, though still falling, remained disturbingly high. The measurable consequences in lost income, unemployment, bankruptcies, and weakened loan portfolios were bad enough. Worse yet, Americans' confidence in strong steady growth and substantial price stability was shattered. The outlook was much as it had been in 1938—a grudgingly slow upturn accompanied by high unemployment and inflation. This dismal prospect (combined, of course, with the memory of Watergate) helped Carter defeat Nixon's successor, Gerald Ford, in 1976.

Jimmy Carter was not cast in the mold of preceding Democratic presidential candidates. Whatever his character strengths or flaws, he was the first postwar Democratic president to come to office as an economic conservative. Unlike Lyndon Johnson, Harry Truman, or even John Kennedy, Carter's orientation was not to throw money and new agencies at the problems of America's disadvantaged. Kennedy and, to a greater extent, Johnson had put a supply-side concept into practice—reducing taxes to spur economic growth so as to increase, not decrease, federal revenues. But somehow the theory had not quite worked out that way. Deficits rose; when the Fed monetized them, inflation followed. The apparent flaws in the economies of the United States and other Western countries undermined the acceptance of Keynesianism. Monetarists blamed the Fed for failing to check money growth. Supply-siders argued that high taxes and excessive government regulation hurt the economy by generating a climate unfriendly to investment, the sine qua non for improving employment, productivity, and income. While not clearly committed to the supply-side thesis, Carter was sympathetic to it. In fact, his administration initiated the deregulation of many segments of the U.S. economy, including depository institutions.

Carter's conservatism, however, did not lead him to support tight money any more than Nixon's had. Like most modern politicians, he wanted economic growth and feared unemployment. Burns was accommodative in hopes of being reappointed; nevertheless, Carter replaced him in 1978 with William Miller. Another president, whatever his philosophical bent, was opting for loose money to forestall recession; and another Fed chairman, theoretically independent of elected officials, was cooperating. Carter and Miller kept the GNP rising, if more slowly than before 1973, and held unemployment in check, though it stubbornly hovered around 6 percent. Inflation, which was at 6 percent, once more began to climb: in 1979 it reached double digits and seemed to be moving out of control. Carter's predicament was excruciating. Many analysts were predicting imminent recession, yet prices kept going up. In desperation, the president appointed a new Fed chairman, Paul Volcker, who was determined to break the pattern he had observed for fourteen years.

In the spring of 1980 Carter and Volcker initiated a joint program of credit restraints, which was so effective that inflation tumbled. But so did the economy, right into a recession. In short order they had reversed course; so had economic growth and inflation. Weighted down by another even more damaging political albatross, the American hostages in Iran, Carter was highly vulnerable to Reagan's campaign attack on his "misery index"—8 percent unemployment plus 12 percent inflation, a horrendous score of 20. Carter had invented this method of chastising a president four years earlier, when Ford's total had been 12, 6 percent each. Reagan not only made much the same domestic criticism of Carter that Carter had made of Ford, but he also offered similar solutions—reduced government spending, less regulation, and sound money. He, like Carter, campaigned not just against the incumbent but against the entire Washington establishment. Reagan, as he so often promised, was determined to get the federal government "off people's backs." Further thrift deregulation was a high priority.

Housing Production, Sales, and Finance

Housing production had not lived up to expectations in the 1960s. Annual starts averaged 1,442,000, 65,000 lower than in the 1950s. For thrifts, whose main business was financing home ownership, another fact was discouraging: late in the 1960s, production of single-family homes had decreased as a percentage of total production. In 1966, for example, it reached 66.9 percent, but fell to 55.3 percent in 1969. Total starts hit a decade low of 1,165,000 in 1966, rose to 1,508,000 in 1968, but dropped again in the following period of recession and tight money, reaching 1,467,000 in 1970. The sales of existing housing, which constituted about two-thirds of savings and loans' financing of single-family homes, were also unspectacular.

The picture in the 1970s, however, was far brighter. Starts averaged 1,548,000, over 100,000 greater than in the 1960s. Production was considerably higher in the first half of the decade, entirely because of a surge in multifamily starts. In 1972 apartment starts exceeded 1 million for the first and only time in U.S. history; indeed, the high level of apartment construction from 1971 through 1973 turned out substantially to exceed demand. Several new sources supplied the money for this production. In response to changes in tax laws and rising income brackets, syndicators and real estate investment trusts were able to raise large sums, much of which found its way into housing. Also, partly for tax reasons (deferral of capital gains on "pooled" mergers), many non–real estate companies acquired builders and provided them with capital to expand production.

Not only did the government induce apartment development indirectly; it greatly increased direct subsidies as well. Once again a supposedly conservative Republican behaved like a liberal. In 1965 subsidized housing, mostly in the form of low-interest loans for new apartment projects, had accounted for 4.1 percent of total residential construction. Since conservatives had consistently objected to the use of submarket rates for loans on the grounds that it disguised the true cost to the government, the Nixon administration designed a new form of support—direct subsidies to mortgage holders. Although these subsidies constituted twenty- to forty-year commitments, only the current year's outlay was counted in the budget; thus, a large number of units could be underwritten at an immediately low cost. As with monetary policy and wage and price controls, the president did not allow ideological consistency to prevent the adoption of government practices that stimulated the economy. In 1970 subsidized housing constituted 29.2 percent of total housing production, a postwar high. And even though this share fell in 1971, at 20.6 percent it was still five times the 1965 level.

Apartments did not account for all the increase in housing starts in the early 1970s. Whereas annual single-family starts had never reached 1 million in the 1960s, from 1971 through 1973 they exceeded this figure, reaching a high of 1,309,000 in 1972. Sales of existing houses also rose: in contrast to the ups and downs of new house production, used-house sales increased steadily from 1970 to 1978, achieving rates far higher than those of the previous decade. The maximum level of 3,986,000 in 1978 was over twice the maximum level in the 1960s.

Extensive overbuilding, mostly in apartments, caused a deep drop in the number of total starts over the next several years. It fell to 1,338,000 in 1974 and to 1,160,000 in 1975, the latter less than half the number in 1972, with the decline as disproportionately in apartments as was the preceding rise. The rebound, however, came quickly and sharply, this time mostly in sales rather than in rental housing. From mid-1975 to 1979 the boom in home sales and production far surpassed any in U.S. history. It was caused by six major factors: (1) the large pool of potential buyers, those born in the baby boom of the late 1950s; (2) the growth of women's participation in the work force, which bolstered family income; (3) an odd demographic factor related to the second, a high rate of divorce, which increased household formation as more women lived alone; (4) inflation, which raised incomes and made the purchase of homes an easy and apparently sound investment decision; (5) lenders, mostly savings and loans, that inadvertently subsidized the purchase of housing; and (6) the introduction of new sources of home financing.

The resultant rise in used-home sales has already been mentioned. Starts did not reach the heights of 1971–1973. In only one year, 1978, did they exceed 2 million, and then just barely. Unlike the first half of the decade, the late 1970s saw a surge, not in construction, but mostly in housing for sale. Apartment starts never surpassed 500,000, and construction in buildings with five or more units averaged only about 20 percent from 1976 through 1979. At no other time in U.S. history had the production of sales housing, new and used, been so strong.

Thrifts

The events from 1967 through 1979 described above fostered not only a continuation and even an acceleration of thrift asset growth but also, until 1978, an apparent reversal of the decline in thrift profitability. In California revived population and economic growth combined with rising inflation to prevent the deep losses that would otherwise have resulted from the overfinanced housing and land inventory of 1966. In 1974 the same problem faced lenders everywhere in the United States, including thrifts; yet thrifts, with some exceptions, were generally not so overexposed now as the ones in California had been eight years earlier. In California, although some associations once again engaged in risky lending, the state's economy was less hard hit this time than the nation's and rebounded dramatically. So bad was the position of several banks and real estate investment trusts (REITs) in other areas, however, that even economic recovery and renewed inflation could not stave off substantial losses. Some of their loans and foreclosed real estate were so far under water that five years of general economic recovery and high inflation could not raise property values enough to cover the loans before the next recession hit. A number of banks, including Chase Manhattan, would have been insolvent had the Fed then chosen the austerity course finally adopted by Volcker in 1981. Many REITs did go broke.

Savings and loans' growth in assets and returns on net worth were impressive indeed. Savings banks, however, did not perform nearly as well, instead continuing their decline in importance. For example, while the number of savings and loans fell to 4,613 in 1980, their total assets rose almost five times, from $130 billion in 1965 to $630 billion in 1980. Savings bank assets also increased in that period, but less than three times, from $59 billion to $172 billion. Thus, by 1980 savings and loans had 79 percent of total thrift assets.

Although virtually all the decline in the number of associations was in state, non-FSLIC-insured institutions, the asset relationship between state and federal savings and loans did not materially change. For example, California companies' share of total savings and loan assets fell from 20 percent to 16 percent; but California stock companies raised their share of state association assets from 63 percent to 80 percent. Furthermore, California savings and loans continued to grow faster in size than other U.S. associations. In 1980 California savings and loans had an average $600 million in assets. Florida savings and loans, with $400 million, came next; Texas, Illinois, and Ohio associations averaged just over $100 million. When only stock companies are counted, the gap in size between those in California and those elsewhere is even greater.

Earnings also went up, though returns on net worth and assets showed less-than-glowing results. For all savings and loans, net income as a percentage of net worth had reached a high of 15.0 percent in 1955. It declined then to 12.4 percent in 1960, 9.8 percent in 1965, and 4.8 percent in 1967. From this low point, return on net worth fluctuated more or less with the course of the economy, rising to 12.1 percent in 1972 and falling back to 7.8 percent in 1975. In the next three years the rebound was especially strong: in 1978 return on net worth hit 14.8 percent, only slightly below the 1955 level. However, it then fell modestly to 12.1 percent in 1979 and precipitously to 2.4 percent in 1980. Return on assets fell to 0.64 percent in 1979 and to 0.13 percent in 1980. The average from 1961 through 1965, in contrast, was 0.80 percent; in the next two five-year periods the average fell to 0.56 percent and then rose to 0.65 percent. In 1978 it climbed to 0.84 percent.

For savings banks, return on assets followed a similar course, remaining substantially below that of savings and loans and actually showing a loss in 1980. Savings bank spreads between deposit and loan rates were constrained more than those of savings and loans, in part because of an onerous usury law in New York. Although California savings and loans continued to show better returns on assets and net worth than those in other states, their relative decline was about the same. In the 1970s they did not come close to reaching the 1962 highs of a 1.9 percent return on assets and a 23 percent return on net worth. In 1980 these percentages fell respectively to 0.5 and 0.8.

This earnings record in and of itself did not demonstrate that a crisis was looming. However, the developments of the late 1970s which lay behind these numbers show clearly that an era for thrifts had ended. Two causes could be found in the way that savings banks and savings and loans operated. First, operating costs rose as a share of assets. In 1950 the percentage for savings and loans was 1.3, and even though it fell to about 1.2 in the 1960s, by 1979 it was back just where it had been thirty years earlier. At savings banks the situation was worse: after remaining constant at under 0.5 percent until 1968, expenses as a share of assets nearly doubled, reaching almost 0.9 percent by 1980. More serious than the change in percentage was the change in direction. Expenses were not only rising as a share of assets but were rising at an increasing rate. Mark Taper, chairman and founder of American Savings and Loan in California, had long ago enunciated his absolute rule that savings and loans could not make a decent profit unless operating costs were kept at or below one percent. The thrift industry had apparently abandoned the Taper doctrine. This would not have been crucial if other factors had allowed thrifts to raise their gross income or their interest rate spread. But in fact the opposite was true.

The second internal factor, the one on which deregulation advocates focused most of their attention, was the maturity mismatch between thrift assets and liabilities. The assets were long, principally thirty-year, fixed-rate home loans; the liabilities, in contrast, were short, mainly passbook, accounts subject to immediate withdrawal. If depositors could get better rates elsewhere, thrifts would either have to raise theirs or suffer disintermediation, which in an extreme case would constitute a run. The Federal Home Loan banks could provide some liquidity, as they had in 1966, 1969–1970, and 1973–1975, but they too had to compete for funds in the market.

In 1976, when the economy was clearly recovering and home sales were beginning to surge, the inflation rate was 6 percent. At that time thrifts were charging 8.5 to 9 percent interest on mortgages, a 2.5 to 3 percent real interest rate. If neither inflation nor the yield curve (the relation between short- and long-term interest rates) changed, thrifts could make a profit, though it was being reduced by mounting expenses. But rising inflation and interest would hurt earnings. If anticipated inflation was higher than current inflation, the real interest rate would be lower than 2.5 to 3 percent. In fact, millions of home buyers—who had never heard the term *real interest rate*—instinctively assumed that the inflation rate would rise. They saw in home mortgages a game that might be called "beat the bank," in which they could borrow money at a zero or even negative real interest rate, but only if they bought a house. Buyers expected values to rise. By providing subsidized financing that could be transferred on resale, lenders guaranteed that value increases would exceed the inflation rate.

Thus, borrowers received an enormous transfer of wealth. This did not harm the government, as long as thrifts had enough net worth. If net worth dropped, however, FSLIC stood to lose a lot of money. Even this would not affect taxpayers as long as FSLIC reserves were sufficient. In fact, the condition of savings and loans had been steadily deteriorating. In 1969 net worth was 7.2 percent of total assets; by 1980 it had fallen to 5.3 percent. These percentages were calculated according to generally accepted accounting principles (GAAP), under which thrifts (and banks) were not, as were most other businesses, required to restate their assets to the lower of cost *or market.* By 1980 inflation and interest rates were both over 12 percent, whereas the average yield on thrift portfolios was 8.8 percent. Thus, the market value of loans was far less than their book value. If thrifts had adjusted the calculation of net worth to reflect the current value of both assets and liabilities in 1980, their net worth would have been −$17.5 billion. Meanwhile, the total reserves of the FSLIC were only $6.5 billion! And as if this discrepancy were not dire enough, it seemed probable in 1981 that inflation and interest rates would rise still further, causing the negative net worth and the current operating losses of thrifts both to get worse.

Even if rates stabilized or fell moderately, the potential for thrift profits was constrained not only by rising operating costs but also by new forms of competition for both savings and home loans. Throughout the 1970s ever-increasing numbers of Americans with ever-increasing amounts of savings became aware that depositing their money in banks or thrifts at rates restricted by government fiat was costing them income. If they were rich or sophisticated enough, they could get higher yields by buying certificates of deposit (CDs), Treasury bills, or commercial paper. For most people, though, these investment opportunities were either unavailable or inconvenient. In 1978 the Home Loan Bank Board allowed savings and loans to meet part of this investment demand by offering money market certificates (MMCs), deposits of $10,000 or more and six- or thirty-month duration at a rate of 0.25 percent above Treasury obligations of the same term. In short order, the amount invested in MMCs soared and by 1980 accounted for 36 percent of all savings and loan deposits. However, principally because of the prescribed term, they were far from satisfactory to most savers. Wall Street and other investors provided a viable alternative in the form of money market mutual funds, which were uninsured and unregulated. These funds first appeared in the early 1970s, but became significant only in 1978, when they accounted for a $34 billion increase in savings, slightly less than the $39 billion increase captured by savings and loans and ten times the amount captured by savings banks.

Competition came not only from money market funds but also from commercial banks and pension funds. In 1971, for example, the thrift share of the combined savings increase of thrift savings deposits, commercial bank savings deposits, money market funds, and pension funds was 29 percent. By 1980 it had fallen to 16 percent. The growing importance of pension funds was, of course, a direct consequence of increasing per capita income and of employee demands for greater security. In addition to paying government insurance for retirement, health, and disability, private companies were required to contribute to and administer, often jointly with unions, their own retirement programs. Throughout the capitalist world, pension funds were the fastest growing repositories of savings—and unlike thrifts or banks, they did not need to advertise or maintain branches.

The growth of pension funds was not a major threat to thrifts as long as they did not invest in home loans, which in the 1960s they did not because of the complexity and lack of liquidity of residential mortgages. In the late 1960s and early 1970s, however, two institutions led pension funds into mortgage investments. The first was the Government National Mortgage Association (Ginnie Mae) with authority to buy FHA and VA loans and issue securities. The high quality of the collateral—government-insured or government-guaranteed mortgages plus the commitment of a federal agency—and the availability of marketable securities or bonds changed pension fund regulations and decisions. Pension funds now could and did provide money for home mortgages through securitization. A second competitor for home loans was the Federal National Mortgage Association (Fannie Mae), a federal agency formed in 1938 to buy FHA and VA mortgages in tight-money periods and subsequently privatized in 1968. In 1970 still another entity, the Federal Home Loan Mortgage Corporation (Freddie Mac), was created to fund and securitize conventional mortgages. While Freddie Mac was established by the Home Loan Bank Board, its stock was owned by savings and loans; they promoted it as a competitor to Fannie Mae and Ginnie Mae, which primarily served mortgage bankers.

These three agencies developed securitization and continued to dominate it. As FHA's and VA's share of total home loans declined, Fannie Mae (which got authority to buy conventional mortgages) and Freddie Mac became the principal wholesale intermediaries, purchasing loans from mortgage bankers, banks, and thrifts and converting them to forms of debt acceptable to pension funds. The reception of securities backed by home mortgages grew as a result of increasing pension fund investment needs as well as a new skepticism about the safety of corporate bonds fostered by the bankruptcy of Penn Central and the near failure of Chrysler and Lockheed. While the old assumption that the obligations of large American corporations were inherently secure was coming into serious question, the record of home mortgages was almost perfect. Foreclosures had sunk to an all-time low. At the same time, private mortgage insurance, first introduced in 1957, had come into widespread use and was being written by some of the country's most prestigious companies, notably Sears. In 1970 only 11 percent of all home mortgages were privately insured; by 1980 38 percent were. Private mortgage insurance permitted lenders to raise loan-to-value ratios on conventional loans to 90 and even 95 percent and drive FHA and VA financing toward insignificance.

The impact of securitization and home lending by federal agencies (mainly Fannie Mae) was still minor in 1970, when securitized mortgages constituted only 1 percent and agency loans 5 percent of total single-family debt. By 1980, however, the securitization share had

risen to 15 percent, and there was every reason to believe that the trend would continue. Freddie Mac and
Fannie Mae, as well as private issuers, were constantly
improving techniques to make their securities more attractive and to market them, not only in the United
States but also abroad. To expand originator deliveries
they were streamlining the buying, packaging, and re-
selling process. In addition, thrifts, banks, and mortgage bankers were experimenting with their own conduits, sometimes to broaden the base of loans that could
be securitized. One limitation of Freddie Mac and Fannie Mae, for example, was their maximum loan amount;
some private pools were therefore designed specifically
to securitize "jumbo" loans, that is, those over the
agency limits.

A love-hate relationship developed between thrifts
and the two agencies, especially the savings and loan
offspring, Freddie Mac. Because the agencies were ex-
empt from securities law registration requirements and
because Fannie Mae retained some federal financial
support, investors gave these two peculiar institutions
"agency status," assuming government liability even
though their instruments specifically denied it. As a result, Freddie Mac and Fannie Mae were able to sell debt
at rates lower than other issuers'. Many analysts con-
tended that both agencies were operationally ineffi-
cient, but even if this was so, private companies found
themselves unable to overcome their creditworthiness
advantage. Insofar as thrifts wanted to function as mortgage bankers—originating loans and selling them—
Freddie Mac and Fannie Mae were extremely useful.
Their lower interest cost could be passed on to bor-

rowers, which thereby enlarged the size of the single-family mortgage market. But if, as had been the tradition, thrifts' primary purpose was to originate loans for portfolio (to be retained as assets, not resold), the agencies that secured loans for resale were new and formidable competitors.

The exponential growth of pension fund assets, concerns about the safety of corporate bonds, the expansion of private mortgage insurance, the excellent performance record of home loans, and the development of securitization attacked the very essence of thrifts: the business of taking in savings and investing them in long-term home loans. When anyone could originate loans and sell them to the agencies and other conduits, or even set up his own channel, the ability to acquire deposits, aided by government insurance, was of little, if any, benefit. Mortgage bankers could get lines of credit to warehouse mortgages for the brief period between funding and resale. Large companies like Lomas and Nettleton and Weyerhaeuser could issue commercial paper for the same purpose; their warehousing interest costs might be slightly higher than thrifts', but they did not have to bear the expense and trouble of regulation or competition for deposits. Thrifts had survived and prospered because they provided American homeowners with cheap and convenient financing. Securitizing mortgages for investment by pension funds, whose money costs were lower than thrifts' and, of even greater importance, whose money was not subject to immediate withdrawal, raised a fundamental question. If this was a better way to supply a thirty-year, fixed-rate home loan, what need did thrifts meet? Was not the burgeoning appetite of pension funds for mortgages and the development of an efficient system to originate and deliver those mortgages about to render thrifts vestigial?

Conclusion

Until the National Banking Act of 1863 commercial banks were chartered only by the states, with the exception of the two national banks, which exercised some central banking functions. After Jackson killed the Second Bank, an era of free banking followed that formed the unusual character of American banking—large numbers of banks, restricted branching, federal control limited by state authority, and progressive abandonment of safe, short-term lending. Neither the National Banking Act nor even the Federal Reserve System could unify or rein in the system.

The economy fulfilled the basic requirement of a capitalist society by delivering rapid and accelerating per capita income growth even as the population multiplied. That a capitalist economy was inherently dynamic and therefore unstable also became clear. As the market mechanism became established and industrialization advanced, income rose, but successive depressions were increasingly severe. Bank failures, both a cause and an effect of depressions, also rose in number and severity.

Thrifts, particularly savings and loans, while small in size compared to commercial banks, were in 1900 already beginning to dominate residential lending. As yet, thrifts had not failed in meaningful numbers during hard times, and for the next thirty years they continued to grow rapidly and became more predominant in the area of banking for which savings and loans had originally been established and in which savings banks had come to play an ever greater role—that of fostering home construction and ownership. With the help of thrifts, almost half of American families owned their own homes by 1930.

The Great Depression of 1929–1932 brought the banking system to its knees and led to substantial savings and loan losses and failures. Savings banks, however, escaped virtually unscathed. The federal government pumped millions of dollars into banks and savings and loans to forestall a total collapse. Bank deposit insurance, having recently failed to protect depositors at the state level, was instituted by the federal government for the first time. Like other New Deal programs, setting up federal deposit insurance constituted a novel political decision. American voters had had their fill of ever more drastic depressions and the attendant bank failures and depositor losses. Providing thrifts with insurance, however, was not necessary simply to guarantee stability; instead it signaled a commitment to continued support for housing, as did the creation of FHA. Along with rejecting uncontrolled cyclicity, the public opted to have the federal government foster home ownership. In a further complication and subdivision of regulatory authority, however, savings and loans got their own agencies—the Bank Board, Home Loan banks, and FSLIC, entirely separate from the Comptroller of the Currency, the Federal Reserve Board, and FDIC, which insured commercial *and* savings banks. Commercial banks and savings and loans could each elect state or federal charters. After a slow start, the institutions with the most deposits joined one of the two insurance agencies; indeed, they could not compete for savings without doing so. By 1980 the maximum amount to which an account could be insured had risen to $100,000.

From the end of World War II until 1973, the general economy and thrifts both grew faster than ever. Yet in the 1950s and 1960s two disturbing trends emerged: thrift returns on net worth and assets peaked in 1955 and then steadily declined; and after 1966, inflation, which had been under 2 percent, began to rise sharply. California savings and loans, which by 1965 had 20 percent of all association assets, operated quite differently from most others. They paid premiums for deposits, aggressively seeking them outside the state, and more than offset the cost of the premiums by charging higher interest rates on home loans and engaging in activities like construction and apartment lending that were riskier but better compensated than home lending. As a result, their profits grew until 1962, reaching a level far higher than that of other associations even in 1955. However, when the state's economic and population growth slackened from 1963 to 1966, many California savings and loans were highly vulnerable to loan losses and so competed for deposits by bidding up interest rates. To prevent a recurrence of such a deposit-bidding contest, the Bank Board quickly imposed interest rate ceilings on savings and loans. Although two large California savings and loans did fail, Vietnam War spending, federal deficits, and monetary accommodation prevented calamity by combining to induce a resurgence of economic growth and inflation.

In the 1970s housing construction and sales boomed in response to favorable demographics, infusions of funds from new sources, continuing (although slower) economic growth, and rampant inflation. As in 1967, inflation prevented thrift losses after the 1973–1975 downturn, the first severe recession since 1937–1938. Some banks and many real estate investment trusts had been so lax that even a high inflation rate could not make their real estate loans and investments secure. Thrift asset growth continued, and in 1978 returns as a percentage of net worth climbed almost to the peak of 15 percent reached in 1955. Nevertheless, as the 1970s came to a close and the next decade opened, the coalescence of several trends, most of which had been long developing, bore ominous portents for thrifts:

1. Operating costs were rising as a percentage of assets, after having declined through the 1950s and 1960s.
2. The ratio of net worth to assets was steadily falling.
3. If fixed-rate loans were adjusted to market values, thrift income statements and balance sheets showed insolvency and current losses. The positive benefit of inflation as a protector against credit risk had been incorporated into the reported financials, but the overvaluation of the assets had not.
4. Inflation was rising and threatened to induce a recession.
5. Thrifts faced mounting competition for savings from money market and pension funds and commercial banks.
6. Securitization was threatening to diminish the ability of thrifts to profitably perform their historical function, that of taking deposits and originating home loans for portfolio.

Regulators, most thrift executives, and industry analysts recognized all these developments. Many of them, however, may not have noticed still another negative trend. With the aging of the baby-boom generation, the demand for housing was about to pass its apex and turn down. Nor could divorce spur demand any longer. In fact, it was more likely to curb it: so many people had separated that recouplings were likely to equal or even exceed divorces.

By the end of 1980 the federal government had already instituted major legislative reform, the Depository Institutions Deregulation and Monetary Control Act, and Ronald Reagan was about to take office. Additional changes seemed imminent, for virtually all the assumptions on which the federal government had based its assertions of the need for a continued and even expanded role for thrifts in the 1930s were being challenged. The deregulatory counterrevolutionaries, who had already transformed the transportation industry, were about to take on depository institutions, especially those that many believed to be sacred cows: savings banks and savings and loans.

4

Deregulation
Critique and Action

Contentions that government will restrain liberty and economic growth are nothing new. In the *Wealth of Nations* Adam Smith catalogued the benefits that accrued when the free market replaced mercantilism. Prior to 1929 government intervention to ease the plight of the disadvantaged was grudging in Germany and England and almost nonexistent elsewhere. Conservatives warned that New Deal programs marked the beginning of the end of capitalism, but in successive decades the apparent blessings of Keynesianism quieted their concerns. The 1970s, however, gave the conservatives a new hearing as inflation surged and productivity slackened. Together, the enemies of big government argued, excessive Fed money pumping, high marginal tax rates, and excessive federal regulation were stifling entrepreneurship and investment, the keys to rising income.

Critical attention was focused on activities in which the government was heavily involved, notably transportation, for which considerable deregulation had already been implemented by 1980. Proposals for reform of the structure of depository institutions and the rules under which they operated had poured out of various commissions since 1937. Most of these proposals, however, suggested not so much radical changes in policy—eliminating deposit insurance or increasing capital ratios, for example—as rearrangements of federal agency jurisdiction. The underlying assumption was that ways should be found to encourage innovation. This implied penetrating the wall between thrifts and commercial banks.

The general critique of government intervention grew louder and more insistent. Yair Aharoni, an Israeli, caught the mood in the title of his book *The No-Risk Society.* In the concluding chapter, "Toward an Age of Humility," he describes what went wrong and why:

> The bill (of government protection) is paid by the entire population in terms of higher taxes, higher prices of goods and services, as well as out-of-pocket expenditures and foregone opportunities for increases in growth. . . . Most of the additional insurance programs were forced on the government by interest groups.[1]

Then he succinctly gives the solution:

> It is time to reconcile the demands for political participation and the calls for more and more public insurance with needs of the individual for a little more competition in the market place, a little lower cost of living, and a stability of prices.[2]

Even those overseeing financial institutions joined the chorus endorsing deregulation. One was Jay Janis, then chairman of the Federal Home Loan Bank Board, who nevertheless advised the soon-to-be-instated Reagan administration to use caution:

> I agree that carefully designed attempts to deregulate certain key industries make a great deal of sense, in terms of increased efficiency and productivity. . . . I would urge that the new leadership not be beguiled by extremist ideology. . . . Now is the time for pragmatism.[3]

Another was Kenneth A. McLean, staff director of the Senate Committee on Banking, Housing, and Urban Affairs, who pointed to "the trend toward deregulation in other sectors of our economy and the generally favorable results flowing therefrom."[4]

The need for deregulation of thrifts was increasingly asserted. In 1976, for example, Thomas J. McIntyre, chairman of the Senate Subcommittee on Financial Institutions, told savings and loan executives what form their businesses would soon have to take: "Thrift institutions must become full-service family financial centers in order to remain competitive in the financial marketplace of the future and to retain their viability as primary suppliers of mortgage financing in this country."[5] The same note was sounded by Fred Balderston, an economist and former commissioner of California Savings and Loans (1963–1965): "Wider investment powers and business authority to engage in consumer lending will enable S&L firms to adapt their operations."[6]

Most of the reasons put forth to explain why thrift deregulation was needed have already been identified: (1) the maturity mismatch between assets and liabilities, a time bomb detonated by the post-1965 rise of inflation and interest rates; (2) competition for savings not only from commercial banks but also from new players, notably money market mutual funds; (3) a savers' revolution—people with more money to invest and more dependent on investment income who were less willing to deposit their money in thrifts (or banks) at low interest rates; (4) advancing technology—electronic funds transfer for example—which brought into question the usefulness of depository branches, of which thrifts especially had opened more in recent years; (5) the potential for reduced demand for housing finance as a consequence of altered demographics; (6) the growing acceptability of the contention that housing had been overly favored by national policy; (7) the increasing percentage of this lower level of demand for residential loans that was being supplied by securitization, mostly through Fannie Mae and Freddie Mac, a system with which thrifts could not effectively compete; and (8) competition from mortgage bankers, several of which were establishing national origination networks and could operate effectively without having access to deposit insurance.

Myriad critics within both the banking industry and academia hammered away at the need for reform. The most important of their proposals involved permitting thrifts to compete for savings by lifting all limitations on what depositories could pay for them. Thus, Regulation Q would be abandoned, as would the mandated deposit rate differential imposed in 1966; on the asset side, thrifts not only would be liberated from restrictions against adjustable-rate lending, but as a matter of policy should limit or entirely avoid making fixed-rate loans, except those to be sold. There had already been considerable change in the character of liabilities. Jumbo ($100,000 or over) certificates of deposit were exempt from interest rate control and money market certificates had become significant savings vehicles. By 1980 thrifts were paying market rates on over half their deposits. Furthermore, since the early 1970s in New England, savings banks and then savings and loans had been authorized to offer NOW (negotiable order of withdrawal) accounts. And since 1975 state-chartered California associations could make adjustable-rate mortgages (ARMs), but only with strict limits on the degree of both annual and lifetime interest rate fluctuation.

No one argued that further deregulation, even if it was enacted immediately, could soon solve the thrift dilemma. Both savings banks and savings and loans held assets consisting primarily of below-market-rate, fixed-rate mortgages, which they could not call (require repayment of). Worse yet, in many cases the loans were assumable without rate change upon resale. A liability arrangement to facilitate future matching could not in and of itself wipe out built-in losses. Furthermore, the availability of fixed-rate loans through securitization and likely homeowner resistance to ARMs (which the California experiment already indicated) would work against restructuring. Whatever was done could at best prevent further mismatching. Insofar as thrifts as a whole had been brought to insolvency by rising inflation and interest rates, their short-term fate would be determined by the economy in general and especially by one federal agency—not their largely captive regulator the Bank Board, but the Fed. Few if any thrift executives, government officials, or academics, aware as they were of the box the industry was in, imagined how much worse—or later, how much better—the inflation–interest rate environment would become. Consciously or unconsciously, they simply made a linear projection of the last fifteen years. Had they reflected on business cycle and interest rate history, had they noticed the political trend both in the United States and in Western Europe, or had they simply believed the assertions of Paul Volcker and Ronald Reagan, they might have sensed that while the so-called crisis would soon get worse, it too, like so many others, would pass.

The other main line of proposed change in thrift operations was to permit diversification. Because mismatching resulted from thrifts holding such a high percentage of their assets in mortgages—over 80 percent in the case of savings and loans—and because securitization reduced the demand for mortgages, thrifts, it was argued, should be allowed and encouraged to enter fields with shorter-term lending requirements, the most obvious being mortgage banking, which would utilize thrifts' capacity to originate home loans. But advocacy went beyond that to include activities such as consumer and commercial lending, heretofore conducted primarily by commercial banks. In the 1970s, as part of the New England experiment, savings banks were allowed to make consumer loans. Since 1973 state-chartered savings and loans in Texas had had similar authority. The results were uninspiring. In Texas, associations had only 3 percent of their assets in consumer loans; in New England the percentage, at 0.6, was even lower.

Consumer lending was an important component of a new concept of the thrift role: they were to become full-service deliverers of financial services to the American family. Other proposed activities included credit cards, trusts, insurance, financial planning, personal credit lines, and second mortgages. The last would least break with thrift tradition, but the rest were products already offered by commercial banks.

Advocacy of full diversification came from several, often conflicting, directions. At one extreme were those critics, usually academics, who thought the whole idea of thrifts as specialized institutions was outmoded. Banks, thrifts, and anyone else who wanted to play, they said, should be permitted and even encouraged to compete. These purists were arguing for a "level playing field," on which the public would get the best and least expensive service. Edward J. Kane, perhaps the most prolific opponent of financial institution regulations, put the case unequivocally: "It is widely recognized that government regulation impedes progress and limits customer satisfaction."[7] He condemned Regulation Q and the historical differential, warning savings and loans of dire results if they continued to seek political protection as housing specialists:

> S&L political alliance with housing could easily backfire against them. If S&Ls insist on seeing their primary function as the financing of homes rather than the earning of profits, it is conceivable that the Federal Home Loan Bank Board could end up converted into a division of the Department of Housing and Urban Development. . . . So far, political efforts to win expanded asset and liability powers have foundered on S&Ls' unwillingness to give up the Reg. Q differential and banks' insistence that S&Ls must pay precisely this price to be "granted" new powers.[8]

Kane had no doubt what thrifts should do: "To take charge of their own salvation S&Ls must recognize that they are primarily in the business of retail banking and only secondarily in the business of home finance."[9] He envisioned a life-and-death struggle: "Small banks and small thrifts are going to have to scramble to survive."[10] Kane was making the classic economic contention that maximum efficiency, to him paramount, was hampered by regulatory protection. He completely rejected government bias toward housing but accepted that thrifts might continue to emphasize it.

Other observers supported thrift consumer lending and related activities as a way to help thrifts fulfill their traditional role. Diversification, they asserted, would enable savings banks and savings and loans to provide home financing by adding to profits, especially in tight-money periods when mortgage demand was low. This position was forcefully articulated by Anthony M. Frank, CEO of Citizens Savings and Loan of San Francisco (now First Nationwide), in a direct confrontation with Kane in 1976:

> Somehow Dr. Kane has it in his mind that savings and loan associations want to be family financial centers, and that these centers will approximate commercial banks. The fact of the matter is that the savings and loan business wants to be able to offer sufficient services so that it can continue to attract the volume of savings necessary to meet the Nation's home mortgage demand. All of the services and all of the powers that have been discussed by our industry in recent years are designed for only one purpose: to enable us to attract and keep savings in order to serve the construction and existing home markets.
>
> What will be required in order to meet our function in this society?

1. Long-term extension of Regulation Q with a rate differential. There is no number 2 because the space between Q and everything else is so great;
3. Authority to offer transaction accounts to our customers;
4. Authority to make consumer loans, only to our loan and savings customers—primarily by means of debit balances for our savings, and by means of consumer-type loans secured by an existing first mortgage loan;
5. Trust powers for middle-income families; and
6. A reasonable mortgage investment tax credit of 5 percent or more.[11]

Many thrift executives, especially those running companies much smaller than Frank's, were even more conservative. Not only did they share Frank's devotion to Regulation Q, but they rejected any diversification besides. What did they know about consumer lending, credit cards, and the like? If such unmet needs existed and such wonderful profits were promised, why were the 15,000 or so commercial banks, which were far more experienced, not filling the gap? Were a handful of theorists and big competitors leading thrifts down a primrose path?

As matters turned out, Kane and Frank each won partial victories. Inflation, high interest rates, money market fund competition, and the savers' revolution had rendered restrictions on deposit rates obsolete. Jumbo CDs and MMCs had wedged the door to liability deregulation open; not only could it not be closed, but it was bound soon to be removed entirely. However much Frank, long a savings and loan manager, may have regretted it, Regulation Q and the historical differential were doomed—the Depository Institutions and Monetary Control Act (DIMCA) of 1980 was more a confirmation of that fact than it was a radical construct. On the other hand, Congress by no means shared Kane's contempt for favorable treatment of housing. On this matter Frank's sentiments were far more in touch with the world of politics than were those of his antagonist.

McLean, of the Senate Committee on Banking, Housing, and Urban Affairs, described the essence of the 1980 act: "The central feature of the financial restructuring provisions of the new law is the six-year phaseout of deposit rate ceilings. At the same time, the law contains a number of measures designed to bolster the earnings and competitive viability of thrift institutions in order to afford them the ability to pay market rates of interest on savings accounts."[12] DIMCA instituted four main reforms:

1. It established the Depository Institutions Deregulation Committee (DIDC) to phase out deposit rate ceilings by 1986. Significantly, of five members, only one, the Bank Board chair, was likely to espouse the traditional thrift position.
2. It authorized NOW accounts for individuals and nonprofit corporations.
3. It authorized federally chartered savings and loans to make commercial real estate loans, consumer loans, and investments in commercial paper and corporate debt securities (up to 20 percent of assets).
4. It authorized credit card lending and trust activities for federal savings and loans.

Frank had lost the battle for retention of Regulation Q and the historical differential, but the new law contained most, if not all, of the provisions he had argued for in 1976. Missing on the liability side was the right to establish money market accounts; with deposit insurance thrifts should be able to compete successfully against nonregulated money market mutual funds. Yet the act went further than he had demanded by permitting investment in commercial real estate loans and corporate debt. Another feature of the law, little noted at the time, was to have serious adverse consequences. Savings and loans had been allowed to invest up to 1 percent of assets in "service" companies, wholly owned subsidiaries that could undertake activities from which the parent was barred. In the 1970s service companies primarily bought and developed real estate. Under the 1980 act all geographic restrictions on service company conduct were removed, and the permitted share of assets that could be invested directly was raised from 1 percent to 3 percent.

As events proved, the most dangerous DIMCA reform was the authorization of commercial real estate loans. Banks and insurance companies were already aggressively offering this kind of financing, and pension funds were buying commercial properties for cash. How did commercial mortgages, historically a high-risk form of lending, solve the maturity mismatch? Were not thrifts, which had no experience in this area, likely to be plagued by commercial bank and insurance company rejects?

Conclusion

As 1980 came to an end, thrifts had no reason for optimism. Events, capped by the passage of the new law, had driven them out of the comforting environment they had enjoyed in the 1950s and early 1960s. What they needed—sharply lower inflation and interest rates, along with strong economic growth and a vibrant housing market—seemed a combination beyond hope. The best they and FSLIC could have realistically expected was a period of stability during which they could restructure their portfolios and learn how to handle their new powers. What they got instead was a wildly gyrating economy, the deepest recession in over forty years, more deregulation, and the go-for-broke administration of the Bank Board.

Thrift managers were, of course, preoccupied with the survival of their firms. If theirs were stock companies and they were shareholders, they stood to lose equity. Even if the institutions survived, the managers' jobs were in jeopardy. Given the paucity of FSLIC reserves in relation to the magnitude of the problem, regulators could reasonably have been obsessed with one question: what would happen if the insurance fund was used up? In fact, this concern got little attention in 1980. It would eventually, but not until very late in the game.

5

The Great Depression Revisited: 1981–1982

The Economy

Ronald Reagan took office in 1981, facing much the same economic dilemma that Herbert Hoover had faced in 1929. In each case a long period of prosperity following a deep recession (1920–1921 and 1973–1975) and the last depression (1893–1896 and 1929–1932) was coming to an end. Housing production had peaked several years earlier (in 1925 and in 1978) and was in rapid decline. Interest rates and prices were rising as the Fed tried, unsuccessfully, to bring inflation down. At the same time, some commodity values were showing weakness. Bank portfolios were precariously loaded with loans on real estate, on stocks (in the 1920s), and on commodities, as well as with loans to foreign countries and to companies badly in need of financial restructuring and modernization. Throughout the world, agricultural and manufacturing overcapacity loomed.

The Reagan administration's response, however, differed from Hoover's in three critical ways. First, instead of raising taxes, it lowered them. Second, while it cut domestic spending, it prevented fiscal drag by increasing military outlays. Third, it avoided trade restrictions like the Hawley-Smoot tariffs of 1930. Even more crucial to Reagan's success were the changes initiated in the 1930s and solidified thereafter: government spending in 1980 accounted for a far higher share of GNP, 33 percent versus 10 percent in 1928; a broad and tightly woven safety net gave most poor, sick, disabled, or unemployed people a fairly high living-standard floor; and deposit insurance and lenient regulatory supervision propped up the financial system. As a consequence, the massive deflation of the 1930s, driven by a collapse of spending power and depositories, did not recur.

Nevertheless, in the two situations the Fed's behavior was remarkably constant. In 1928 it began tightening the money supply to rein in resurgent inflation, a policy not reversed until 1931. In 1980 Volcker backed off a similar course, but resumed it the following year. The Fed then relentlessly fought to arrest an apparently out-of-control inflationary spiral. Many condemned the central bank for causing the 1981–1982 recession; yet it did not do so then any more than it had caused the one in 1929. In both instances, the economic downturns were not the result of monetary policy, which could only affect their timing and severity, but the concluding stage of a long-wave business cycle. However, the 1981–1982 recession demonstrated that substantial modifications to capitalism—underwriting banks and thrifts, providing a safety net, and raising government spending's share of total economic activity—could forestall or perhaps even prevent another depression. In 1981 Volcker might have held off the start of the downturn for a few months by being less restrictive; he certainly could have mitigated its severity. But because of his commitment, perhaps even obsession, to jam the inflation genie back into the bottle, he did neither. If he succeeded, interest rates would follow inflation's decline.

As 1982 came to a close, there were indications that the storm was over. The economic downturn appeared to have hit bottom a few months earlier, and both interest rates and inflation had started to fall as the Fed finally let up on the brakes. For thrifts the uncertainty was still excruciating. Would the Fed stay on its course? If so, how long would it take before disinflation set in, and how far would it go? Could thrifts survive a transition from high to low inflation and interest rates?

Housing

Housing starts and sales, both new and existing, had peaked in 1978; the decline was modest the following year but sharp in 1980. Starts went from 2,020,000 in 1978 to 1,292,000 in 1980, a drop of 36 percent. In contrast to the trend in previous downturns, starts of sales housing fell faster than starts of rental units. The fall in sales of new housing, −40 percent, was even greater; sales of existing houses did slightly better, declining 25 percent. Yet the plunge continued. Starts reached postwar lows in both 1981 and 1982, 1,084,000 and 1,062,000 respectively. From 1980 to 1982 sales of new houses fell 25 percent, and of existing houses, 33 percent.

The cyclical decline of housing demand and starts was especially steep because of unprecedentedly high interest rates. The prime rate hit its peak, 20.5 percent, in mid-1981 and then fell sharply. By the end of 1982 it was down to 11.5 percent, its level in June 1979. Conventional mortgage rates did not rise so much, averaging 14.39 percent in 1981, but neither did they come down so sharply. In 1982 their average rose slightly, to 14.73 percent. As 1983 began, though, home loan rates were also falling.

The interest rates just cited were on institutional mortgages. However, so high had rates gotten that for the first time in almost a century a significant number of home sellers took private mortgages as partial payment. This was especially the case in states like California where lenders could not enforce due-on-sale clauses. Buyers assumed the existing debt and sellers received second mortgages. Had this practice not been widespread, home sales and production would have been even lower. Despite rises in house prices, the dollar volume of institutional single-family mortgages originated fell almost 50 percent from its 1979 peak of $187 billion, to $97 billion in 1982.

Thrifts

The number of savings banks and savings and loans continued to shrink in 1982, the former from 323 in 1980 to 315 and the latter more sharply from 4,613 to 3,825. (In one respect the two types of thrift moved in opposite directions: savings and loans continued to open branches, the total number of which rose from 16,733 in 1980 to 18,712 in 1982, whereas for savings banks the number fell from 3,152 to 2,777.) Despite steep drops in mortgage originations and the number of institutions, total thrift assets continued to rise, from $630 billion to $708 billion for savings and loans and from $172 billion to $174 billion for savings banks. In earnings, however, the story was quite different. For the first time since the 1930s, the savings and loan industry as a whole not only lost money but lots of it, $4.6 billion in 1981 and $4.3 billion in 1982. These are aftertax figures: pretax losses were over $1.5 billion more each year. For savings and loans the highest postwar return on net worth was 15 percent, achieved in 1955 and again in 1978. The negative returns in 1981 and 1982 were even higher, −15.44 and −16.13 percent respectively. The comparable results for savings banks were slightly worse, −15.97 percent and −15.62 percent. In the same two years the return on assets was −0.7 percent and −0.6 percent at savings and loans and −0.93 percent and −0.78 percent at savings banks.

These terrible losses were caused, of course, by a continuation of the trend of the previous few years: interest spreads declining and eventually becoming negative. The average interest rate on savings and loan deposits rose from 8.75 percent in 1980 to 11.19 percent in 1982. The rise for savings banks, from 8.03 percent to 9.60 percent, was not quite so bad. These higher rates were still insufficient to maintain thrift deposits, however. For seven straight quarters starting in January 1981, savings and loans experienced total net outflows of $45.7 billion. Only borrowings from Federal Home Loan banks enabled them to survive.

The negative thrift income understates reality, because GAAP accounting did not require adjustment of assets to market values. In 1981, as losses mounted and net worth began to disappear, the Bank Board went further in fostering the inaccurate depiction of thrift finances by encouraging the adoption of new and ingenious regulatory accounting principles (RAP). RAP accounting could not be used by stock companies reporting to their shareholders, but it was available to mutuals, many of which embraced it. One gimmick allowed institutions to sell submarket interest loans at far less than book value and to spread the loss over many years. An even more compelling scheme, sanctioned by GAAP, fostered mergers. The buyer could reduce low-interest-rate loans to market value; the loss was offset by "goodwill," an asset again written off over a long time. Almost as if by magic, association losses disappeared. Still another method of bolstering the image of health came into use when FSLIC issued capital notes that could be counted as net worth. Here the regulators were not just permitting but actually promoting a new form of accounting designed to alter the financial statements savings and loans submitted to show compliance with regulatory guidelines. Carried to an extreme, RAP accounting would guarantee that no matter what an insured institution did and no matter how bad its condition, it could avoid being in violation of FSLIC insurance requirements. Even GAAP allowed the painting of a deceptively rosy picture. To make compliance even easier, FSLIC reduced the required net worth of savings and loans from 5 percent to 4 percent, and then to 3 percent.

Competition for both savings and residential loans mounted relentlessly. In 1981 the deposit situation appeared virtually hopeless as the thrift share of the total annual increase in financial assets held by themselves, commercial banks, pension funds, and money market funds fell from 16 percent to 8 percent. Money market funds were the principal beneficiary of the thrift runoff, increasing their deposits from $29.2 billion in 1980 to $107.5 billion the next year. However, as short-term interest rates fell in 1982 and thrifts began to compete using their new liability powers, disintermediation ended and the cost of funds began to recede.

On the asset side, the situation was far less encouraging. In 1980, when total institutional mortgage originations were $258 billion, federal agencies and mortgage pools together purchased $36 billion, or 14 percent. In 1981, as with thrifts, their funding dropped while their relative position remained constant. In 1982, however, when total originations fell to $154 billion, agencies and pools accounted for $79 billion, or 51 percent of the total. Thrifts hoped to replace lost net worth with earnings generated by growth. Securitization, especially when it went through mortgage bankers, threatened this strategy.

The Regulators

No American president since Andrew Jackson had entered office with a sense of mission as great as Ronald Reagan's. Franklin D. Roosevelt won an equally smashing victory and faced a far worse domestic situation, but he did not bring to the White House a lifetime commitment to roll back the work of his predecessors. However much Reagan may have given in to political pressure as governor of California, and however much he would do so in the future, his ideological conviction remained clear and strong. He was riding a tide of deep public distrust of the federal government's creeping intrusion into all aspects of life, especially the economy. Carter's election had signaled the new national mood, but Carter was, in the Reaganites' view, trapped by a constituency addicted to federal largesse.

The new president inevitably appointed reformers to high positions, rather than defenders of the status quo. From Donald Regan at Treasury came a supply-side budget as he and his boss rammed a controversial reduction in tax rates through a skeptical Congress. From James Watt at Interior came an attack on environmental rules that obstructed economic development. Shaking up depositories was a high priority, but Volcker, a term appointee, whose Fed was the dominant force in bank regulation, remained cautious. Banks were too weak, he claimed, to handle drastic liberalization.

But there was no such obstacle at the Bank Board. As its new head, Reagan chose Richard T. Pratt—young, physically imposing, intelligent, and fearless. A professor of finance and a consultant to savings and loans, Pratt was, like his junior partner, FSLIC director Brent Beesely, from Utah, the home state of Jake Garn, the new chair of the Senate Committee on Banking, Housing, and Urban Affairs. For the first time since the 1950s, Republicans controlled the Senate. Garn was determined not to let this rare opportunity pass. Pratt, an advocate of unshackling financial institutions and letting the market have its way, seemed the right man in the right place at the right time. Backed by a popular and supportive president and a key Senate ally, Pratt set out to drive thrifts into the modern world—whether they liked it or not.

The centerpiece of Pratt's regime was legislation advancing deregulation. As a member of DIDC, he supported the rapid removal of Regulation Q and the historical differential, instead of adopting a traditional go-slow position. In 1982 Congress passed the Garn–St. Germain Depository Institutions Act, which further expanded thrift powers. The two main changes applicable to liabilities authorized thrifts to set up money market accounts and to take demand deposits from businesses. Far more significant were the extensions of investment opportunity, including (1) doubling the maximum percentage of assets in commercial real estate loans and (2) allowing commercial loans of up to 10 percent of assets.

While the federal government was removing long-established restrictions on thrift conduct, so were key states. By the end of 1982, for example, state-chartered savings and loans in California, Texas, and Florida had gained a very wide latitude, especially in the deployment of funds. In theory at least, they could hold all of their assets in directly owned real estate. For federally chartered associations, in contrast, the maximum funds allowable in directly owned real estate, to be carried by their service subsidiaries, was 3 percent of total assets— still, this was more than the book, let alone the true, net worth of many of them.

Greatly expanded thrift powers and the prospect of both an economic recovery and some fall in interest rates made savings and loan charters very attractive. Being able to form, with as little as $1 million in capital, a new association not burdened by old, low-interest-rate mortgages and having the right to offer depositors federal deposit insurance and a net-worth-to-asset ratio of as little as 3 percent seemed too good to be true. Whether choosing to start from scratch or to buy an existing association, real estate developers, syndicators, mortgage bankers, and many entrepreneurs with no particular specialty immediately sensed opportunity, especially in states where economic growth was rapid and regulations were extremely permissive.

There were risks, of course, but the incredible leverage justified taking them. The owners could lose only their original capital; the rest belonged to FSLIC, Treasury, or the depositors. The circle was complete. A century and a half after Jackson ushered in free banking, thrifts, which had been brought under the federal umbrella to ensure their continuing role as safe residential lenders, were given a nearly blank check. The most improvident country banker in the nineteenth century was never allowed to offer government-guaranteed deposits, maintain 3 percent net worth (which could be arrived at through dubious accounting), and invest at will.

Deposit insurance gave the federal government potential regulatory authority it never had before 1933. But the authority had to be exercised. In 1981 FSLIC could have suspended approval of all applications for new charters or acquisitions of existing ones until the thrift industry's crisis passed, allowing those wishing to enter the field to do so only if they took over troubled associations and provided new capital and strong management. In fact, however, it followed exactly the opposite course. In 1981 and 1982 FSLIC approved sixty-one new charters in California alone. In addition, it permitted scores of other, mostly small, associations to transfer control to operators who had every intention of gambling with government funds and in some cases even stealing them. If Pratt was willing to let them sell U.S. Treasury debt, at whatever price, and under whatever terms they chose, using the proceeds to make high-risk

loans and even buy property for development or play securities markets, with 33-to-1 or greater leverage and no
personal liability, he would get plenty of takers.

Pratt and his Salt Lake City sidekick, Brent Beesely,
FSLIC's director, were trying to cope with hundreds of
associations that were already insolvent or bound to
reach that sorry condition in the near future. For the
first thirty-five years of its existence, FSLIC had liquidated only a handful of savings and loans, mostly in Illinois in the mid-1960s. It had had to provide financial
assistance to 130 mergers, the principal method for han-
dling a troubled association. But the total outlays, $344
million, were insignificant in relation to the total assets
involved. In the 1970s, for example, whereas FSLIC's
average annual cost for assistance was $23.5 million,
total assets in 1979 were $579 billion. Until 1980 the
size of the insurance fund was not given much thought.
Even the cost of assisting mergers that year—$167 mil-
lion—was in and of itself no cause for concern. However, when it exceeded $1 billion in both 1981 and 1982,
an alarm bell went off.

Current and estimated costs of assisting forced mergers were but the tip of an iceberg. The reported net
worth of all savings and loans in 1982 was about 3.5 percent of assets, which included the adjustments to RAP
accounting. Had RAP accounting not been used, the figure would have been lower: even if the more favorable
interest rates obtaining by the end of the year were used
in the calculations, market value net worth was negative. Yet the actual amount of total net worth was not
available in any case to solve FSLIC's problem. Many institutions had real, positive net worth. It was inconceiv-
able that more than a modest share, if any, of healthy

associations' capital could be tapped to cover the obligations of insurance coverage.

Knowing that the FSLIC fund was minuscule in relation to the cost of closing currently insolvent associations, Pratt and Beesely might have given the president and Congress a calculation of the funds necessary to do so and requested the required appropriations. Instead they invented artificial accounting devices to mask the situation, encouraged mergers in the hopes that they would improve operational quality, and hoped that a better environment—lower interest rates and economic recovery—combined with skillful use of new powers by thrifts would, if not bail the associations out entirely, at least bring the number of closings and their ultimate cost to manageable levels.

Pratt expected accelerated consolidation within the industry. Fewer, larger firms, he argued, would be more efficient. Mergers, then, were not just a way to apply accounting gimmickry but a way to rationalize an archaic industry. However, many firms were in such bad shape, owing to both submarket rates and low-quality loans, that merger was infeasible. These associations FSLIC took over, to keep them alive: liquidation of even a fraction of such associations would have exhausted the insurance fund. Larger institutions in selected metropolitan areas were identified as "phoenixes," into which smaller companies were merged, with FSLIC installing its own boards of directors and management.

Initially the agency sold phoenixes at modest assistance cost, allowing a company outside the industry to make the acquisition. The most logical purchaser was a commercial bank prohibited by law from operating in a desirable market. Thus Citicorp became a major savings and loan owner by purchasing companies in Chicago, San Francisco, Texas, and Florida. The same device permitted solvent savings and loans to cross state lines: First Nationwide, Home Savings, and Great Western, all large California stock companies, quickly bought associations in the Midwest and East from FSLIC to expand their geographic scope.

Propping up savings and loans by permitting them to function with zero or negative net worth, arrived at by RAP accounting, avoided precipitating a battle within the administration, with Congress, and with the industry. Nevertheless, Beesely, nicknamed "Dr. Doom," was often criticized for being too harsh. Healthy institutions were ambivalent. They did not like FSLIC's policy because it increased deposit and lending competition; but they feared the public's reaction to a wave of closings— and that they too might fall below mandated net worth and desire lenience.

Although the Bank Board's conduct was tolerated, if not supported, as 1982 came to a close, disquiet arose. Creative accounting deferred, but could not permanently eliminate, losses. Goodwill had to be written off, and loans from Home Loan banks and FSLIC had to be repaid. The first profits of an association with little or no net worth went to cover old losses. Only then could earnings boost net worth ratios, which eventually had to reach 3 percent or more. Management facing this dilemma had no choice but to push growth.

One nonpolitical argument for keeping insolvent associations afloat involved liquidation cost. Realizing maximum proceeds from assets or businesses targeted for disposition is sometimes accomplished only over several years. Immediate sale of property and payment of liabilities may drastically reduce proceeds. However, if those managing such a "staged workout" benefit only by generating substantial profits *and* have access to unlimited funds, the dangers are immense. A private corporation would gain from success, but for FSLIC it was a one-way street. Whereas managers and shareholders would reap the rewards of success, the resultant net worth would be of little or no help to the agency. Associations that failed could leave FSLIC with obligations several times the loss that would have accrued from immediate liquidation. Managers need not violate any laws and would represent themselves and any existing shareholders quite properly by taking high risks to reach for profits. They would receive the gains; the government would bear the losses.

Pratt understood the potential pitfalls. Remarkably, he described them in public, at a conference in December 1982:

> The Federal Savings and Loan Insurance Corporation, which has been a substantial regulator and has participated in this deregulation, will be exposed to operating risks such as have never occurred in the past. Assuming rates stay down, the maturity mismatch and thus the interest rate risk can be expected to decline; the operating risks, however, can be expected to increase substantially.[1]

And then in one of the most extraordinary statements ever made by a regulator, he advised his audience, mostly California Savings and Loan executives, how to run an association to beat the system:

> One approach would be to start 10 or 15 thrift institutions or commercial banks and engage in the

most risky activities legally allowed. If you believe that return is related to risks, the expected value of your returns would be higher than under any other approach, while at the same time, you could buy your funds on a risk-free basis through offering U.S. government obligations in the form of insured savings accounts. That is a scenario that we, as regulators, and that you, as management, are going to have to operate under, because that opportunity is a realistic one.[2]

Pratt went on to contend that there was only one way for the government to defend itself: by overhauling deposit insurance. "The flat rate premium, independent of risk, in a deregulated economy seems to me a pattern for disaster."[3] Until this could be done, he concluded, almost as an afterthought, "the insurer must be the regulator."[4] But what objective was important enough to justify the risks? The answer was market efficiency:

The cost of regulation exists out in the economy, and there is probably a leverage factor of a thousand to one, or whatever it might be. The costs imposed on the American people by the FSLIC's existence are not the costs of running FSLIC. Rather the costs are the effects of its regulation and the way it affects the marketplace in which the people of America must deal.[5]

Pratt, who had entered office "hardly thinking about deposit insurance,"[6] had now become obsessed with its distortions. His view was shared by a host of deregulation devotees, among them Edward J. Kane.[7] Most of these believers were academics, free and even obligated to criticize and propose ideal constructs. Pratt, however, was a public official coping with the real world. He had pushed dramatic legislative and administrative expansion of industry powers without first asking for and getting what he himself claimed was an essential precondition: the abandonment or substantial reform of deposit insurance.

In one of his final acts as Bank Board chairman, Pratt personally supervised the preparation of a report, *Agenda for Reform,* submitted to the House and Senate banking committees on March 23, 1983. The entire subject was deposit insurance. In page after page this incredible document identified the dangerous path down which Pratt had led the Bank Board. On the general risk it said:

> Under the system in place today the federal government shares in any losses, while gains accrue entirely to those who have interests in depository institutions. A rational course of action in these circumstances is for the firm to engage in activities that may be excessively risky.[8]

On how mergers increase potential costs to FSLIC by covering uninsured creditors:

> If uninsured depositors are to exert market discipline, it is imperative that they perceive their deposits to be at risk. Most failures of FSLIC-insured institutions have been solved through some kind of merger that protects all creditors of the failed institution. Although such policies may minimize agency costs and financial market disruption, they also lessen the concern of uninsured depositors with respect to the riskiness of individual depository institutions.[9]

On pressure from agencies and securitization:

> In late 1982 the competition came principally from purchasers of mortgages in the secondary mortgage markets, and they were purchasing long-term fixed-rate mortgages. . . . As long as S&Ls continue to offer liabilities with short maturities and long-term mortgages with fixed rates, both they and FSLIC will be exposed to substantial rate risk. Yet if S&Ls refrain from offering long-term fixed-rate mortgages when other investors with long-term liabilities are willing to buy them, they will lose their market share.[10]

On the competitiveness of commercial and consumer lending and the lack of association expertise:

> Both the commercial and consumer lending markets are already very competitive. Savings and loans associations have no particular expertise in these markets and no particular comparative advantage over the commercial banks and finance companies that already serve them.[11]

On how the regulators had become hamstrung:

> Although the deregulation of the past few years was a necessary response to marketplace innovations, it also substantially limited the ability of regulatory agencies to constrain the risk-taking of insured institutions.[12]

And on the dangers that risk-taking implies:

> Moreover, this has occurred at a time when there are a number of insured institutions that are operating with impaired capital and have strong incentives to engage in very risky investments. In the

light of the competitive pressures that the industry will face in the next few years, this deregulation could result in substantial losses.[13]

When this report was published, the prime rate had fallen another full point, to 10.5 percent, and recovery from the recession seemed assured. Acknowledging these developments, the authors made a confession that was astounding in the light of future events:

> The recent problems of the savings and loan indus-
> try, and so of the FSLIC, reflect the effects of ex-
> traordinary interest rate movements on a vulner-
> able industry. These problems could have been
> handled with minimum losses to the insurance
> fund had FSLIC closed S&Ls when their net worth
> approached zero. However, such a policy would
> have resulted in the closing of every S&L in the
> country.[14]

The last sentence was patently false. Hundreds of associations had net worths of over 3 percent under GAAP accounting, and far more were at 0 percent to 3 percent. If FSLIC could have liquidated insolvent institutions at little or no cost, what were the reasons for not having done so? Did securitization not suggest that fewer thrifts with fewer assets were needed to finance housing? Could commercial banks and money market funds not supply depositors with all the needed services? Could commercial banks and investment bankers not handle the consumer and commercial loan demand? If all Pratt and the Bank Board were up to was turning thrifts into commercial banks, when there were already too many of them, what was the point?

Conclusion

Pratt left the government to join Merrill Lynch in April 1983. His was a curious legacy. In public statements, culminating with *Agenda for Reform*, he had described the calamities that could result from the course he had charted. He had bet that a favorable economic climate and prudent thrift management would mitigate the risks and that the cause of the government's trouble, deposit insurance, would be abolished or changed beyond recognition. Despite the steady subsequent castigation of deposit insurance, there was not then nor is there now the slightest chance of its being altered substantially, let alone canceled. Pratt's successors were blessed with an economy beyond their wildest dreams. Interest rates fell steadily for over four years. At the end of 1986, the prime rate was 7.5 percent and one-year Treasury bills were under 6 percent, levels not seen since the early 1970s. GNP has risen in every quarter since the autumn of 1982, at an annual average rate of about 2.5 percent. Yet FSLIC is in far worse shape than it was when Pratt left office. Somehow defeat was snatched from the jaws of victory.

6

Disaster Strikes: 1983–1987

The Economy and Housing

The recovery years 1983–1986 and 1933–1937 bore considerable resemblance to one another. The great difference between the two periods lay not in the Fed's policy but in the government's fiscal and regulatory role during the preceding downturns. Only after recession had taken a heavy toll was monetary restraint abandoned. From then on, in both instances, the central bank, aided in the 1980s by an influx of foreign funds, supplied money generously. In 1931, when no safety net existed, when government spending was less than 10 percent of GNP, and when banks were failing en masse, the Fed could not reverse the deflationary tide. Business activity went into free-fall. In 1982 increases in military spending and tax cuts combined with existing federal programs to enlarge deficits and prevent a recurrence of the depression of the early 1930s, or for that matter of the depressions of the nineteenth century. Some observers contend that economic fluctuations were less sharp in the mid-1980s also because the service sector, which is less volatile than the manufacturing sector, accounts for a much higher share of GNP.

Although recovery in the 1980s began at a far higher level than it did in the 1930s, the economy was buffeted in both periods by similar countervailing pressures. Government spending and deficits, as well as monetary expansion, bolstered demand and inflation. But at the same time, widespread agricultural and industrial overcapacity curbed demand and was deflationary. In both periods inflationary forces were stronger than deflationary forces, and prices rose. Yet the money supply climbed faster than the inflation rate, because money velocity slowed down; the disparity was especially great in the 1980s as people made an adjustment, sometimes painfully, to disinflation. Had the reduction in velocity been clearly recognized, the Fed might have accommodated further, thereby easing the burden of high real interest rates. In the end, though, it confronted a dilemma not present in the 1930s. With the domestic savings rate at an all-time low and with the country buying far more abroad than it sold, the budget deficit could not be funded internally. As a result, U.S. interest rates became heavily dependent on foreign behavior. American central bankers thus now reside not only in Washington but also in Tokyo and Bonn.

In the 1980s as never before, banks and thrifts became a major government instrument in offsetting deflationary forces. When lenders called loans in the 1930s, the dollar's increased value exceeded the reduction in nominal debt and a vicious deflationary cycle ensued. In the

1980s, encouraged by regulators, lenders did just the opposite by recasting uncollectible loans and, instead of adopting restrictive credit standards, by aggressively expanding debt. Accounting gimmickry, lower net worth ratios, and liberally administered regulations fostered the ambitious financing of new projects and refinancing of old ones. Refinancing would not have greatly affected the economy if the amount of debt had remained the same, but lenders often provided additional funds in the process. The increments were used for investment in new enterprises or for consumption, thus underpinning demand and helping to counter deflation.

Real estate lending was the principal device for monetizing equities. Mortgage bankers (including thrifts and banks acting in this capacity) and thrifts sought to offset amortization and repayment and expand portfolios to cover old losses and rising overhead. Some borrowers bought existing houses, thereby sharply increasing debt; others refinanced, investing or spending the proceeds; still others bought new homes. The last did so in sufficient numbers to bring annual starts almost to the levels of the late 1970s. The two dismal years 1981 and 1982 were followed by a production surge in 1983, when starts reached 1.7 million units and single-family starts again passed 1 million. In the next three years starts averaged over 1.75 million and topped 1.8 million in 1986. Sales of existing housing also rebounded strongly. After falling from almost 3 million in 1980 to less than 2 million in 1982, the number of existing units sold jumped back to 2.7 million in 1983 and approached 3.5 million by the end of 1986.

The resurgence of home construction, in total contrast to the sudden abeyance of the 1930s, contributed heavily to overall economic growth. At least for the time being, it demonstrated the efficacy of federal budgetary, monetary, and regulatory policies. By propping up the banking system in general and thrifts in particular and by supporting the agency status of Freddie Mac and Fannie Mae, the government achieved in the 1980s what it had not in the 1930s—a strong rise in residential building, which not only continued to improve the country's housing standards but also stimulated an inherently sluggish economy. Under Ronald Reagan, an archconservative who came to office decrying federal intervention, Keynesian prescriptions to prevent another cyclical collapse like the one in 1929–1932 and to foster more rapid recovery to full employment (which fell from over 10 percent in 1982 to under 6 percent in 1987) got their test. To date, the prescriptions have worked.

As the decade began, both ardent supporters and hard-nosed skeptics of thrift deregulation expressed dark apprehension about housing production in the 1980s and the "affordability" problem. Kenneth Rosen, a highly respected and oft-quoted real estate economist, exemplifies this concern: "The final element of the crisis facing the thrift industry [in December 1980] is the unprecedented political attack on the housing industry and the specialized housing finance system. At a time when housing construction is at its second lowest level in three decades and when the thrift industry is barely surviving, it is extremely poor public policy to undermine further an already weak system."[1] Apparently rejecting any possibility that interest rates would soon turn down, Rosen depicted thrifts as having "an unrealized portfolio loss of $100 billion." He demanded further deregulation, which the Garn–St. Germain act delivered, but thought that even if deregulation came, what he and so many others described as a housing crisis would remain. Rosen called for a rebuilding of the "housing and finance coalition . . . if we are to meet [the need of] the post–World War II boom generation in the 1980s."[2]

In actuality, annual housing starts from 1980 through 1986 averaged about 1.5 million, halfway between the levels of the 1960s and 1970s. In 1987 starts were almost 1.7 million. Given the steep reduction in 1980, 1981, and 1982, which resulted from an inevitable cyclical downturn and high interest rates, and the decline in population growth, which weakened demand, that was a respectable performance. In fact, as the 1980s wore on, attention shifted from a housing shortage to the concern of the 1960s, overproduction, which was reflected in rising vacancy rates. In late 1987 Rosen was informing clients that apartment vacancy rates exceeded 7 percent, a level not reached since 1966, and that demographics, in major part because recouplings were outstripping divorces, would dampen housing demand.

Thrifts

Thrifts were, of course, delighted that home production and sales snapped back. However, their share of residential financing continued to recede. Ironically, after earlier declaring a housing finance shortage, Rosen told thrift executives in 1986 what their daily struggle demonstrated—that securitization was taking a bigger piece of the home mortgage pie. Securitization reached $110.8 billion in 1986, 58.3 percent of all single-family loans originated. The thrift share of outstanding mortgages had fallen from over 53 percent in 1975 to under 40 percent. "Other" holders, which in 1900 had meant private individuals and companies but which now meant primarily pension funds, had raised their percentage of residential mortgages from 17.7 in 1975 to 45.2 in 1986.

Thrifts could and did originate loans and resell them for securitization, even though in doing so they faced relentless competition from mortgage bankers. Nevertheless, as interest rates fell in 1985 and 1986, after a considerable upward spike in 1984, mortgage banking became a profitable undertaking. Its practitioners captured a double benefit while holding loans for resale: first, they got an interest spread; second, if, as was often the case, they did not hedge fixed-rate loans and rates fell during the holding period, they gained from rising values. Furthermore, declining rates reduced the negative spread of old portfolios and in some instances turned them positive.

A few small thrifts avoided portfolio lending by operating entirely as mortgage bankers, channeling originations through an insured institution. For them, thrift ownership simply provided warehousing facilities that they hoped would be more efficient than credit-line borrowing. But most firms, especially large ones, could not generate enough loans for resale to operate in this fashion; they had to use insured deposits for spread-lending. Three potential portfolio strategies were available to them: (1) making only short-term commercial, consumer, construction, or development loans; (2) making fixed-rate loans to capture the initially wide spread relative to variable-rate loans and hope rates would fall and the yield curve would widen; and (3) making ARMs, either by originating or by buying them.

The experience of the 1970s and the temporary reversal of the interest rate decline in 1984 made fixed-rate lending seem foolhardy; indeed, it was publicly condemned by virtually every commentator, regulator, investment banker, and thrift executive. Yet as matters turned out, holding fixed-rate loans would to date have been highly profitable—even if the increase in interest rates after early 1987 is taken into account—since the average cost of funds fell from its high of 11.4 percent in 1982 to 7 percent in 1987, the same as it was in late 1978. However, few firms stuck to fixed-rate lending alone; it was just too unfashionable. Virtuous managers were supposed to use the breathing space provided by lower interest rates and surging originations to "restructure" (convert portfolios from fixed to variable). They were keenly aware that doing so might mean sacrificing near-term profits, but most institutions moved strongly in that direction.

California, where ARMs had been offered since 1975, became even more predominant in the thrift industry and led the nation in variable-rate lending. In 1986 twelve of the nation's fourteen largest savings institutions, each with assets of $11 billion or more, were in the state, and its associations accounted for almost 40 percent of all savings and loan financing. Virtually all large California institutions concentrated on ARMs. Some, like Home Savings of America and World Savings, eschewed fixed-rate loans entirely. Others made them, but only when they could be resold immediately or matched with Federal Home Loan bank borrowing. When interest rates rose and the yield curve widened in 1987, many lenders in other parts of the country emulated the giant California companies.

It has become standard practice for thrifts to include in their annual reports a "gap" analysis showing how closely the terms of maturities and liabilities coincide. Ideally, the gap is zero. Little attention, however, focuses on two potentially adverse consequences of ARMs. First, lenders acquired ARMs at the cost of a considerable reduction in immediate spreads. Second, in their zeal to wean borrowers from fixed-rate loans, ARM lenders have softened credit standards.

Thus, while ARMs are a wonderful idea, in practice they are seriously flawed. Competition from mortgage bankers, originating for ultimate securitization, mostly through Freddie Mac and Fannie Mae, and competition among thrifts kept spreads under downward pressure. As pension funds reduced their yield requirements (the spread over Treasury bills), as mortgage bankers shaved their margins, and as overall interest rates fell, homeowners expressed their preference for fixed-rate loans. To coax them into choosing ARMs, thrifts offered true rates as much as 2 percent below fixed rates and gave "teasers"—first-year rates another 1 percent or more lower and both annual—and lifetime "caps" (thirty-year interest-rate ceilings). Many institutions qualified borrowers at the teaser rate, thereby making loans far larger than if the rate had been fixed. Most California associations indexed their ARMs to the Eleventh District [Home Loan Bank] Monthly Average Cost of Funds, at a spread of 2 to 2.25 percent. If their own money costs were lower than the average and if they could hold operating costs below 1.5 percent of assets, they might generate a pretax return of 1 percent of assets. This profit base could be broadened by successful diversification into consumer, construction, and commercial lending; credit cards; direct development; and other fields. But what of thrifts whose operating and money costs were above the average? They could not afford the luxury of transforming themselves into portfolio ARM lenders. For them, gambling on fixed-rate loans, on diversification, or on both was not just supplementary, it was central. How else could they generate decent returns on net worth—if they had any—and bring it to an acceptable level?

With thrifts having such a low overall net worth ratio at the end of 1982 and with rising competition from securitization, economists might reasonably have expected slow asset growth, or even a decline, and a brutal attack on operating costs—the only sensible way to increase spreads and, therefore, net worth ratios. Assuming prudence in thrifts' utilization of their expanded asset powers, especially in the face of disinflation and rising commercial and residential real estate vacancies, what other course was conceivable? However, if the government underwrote the industry with deposit insurance, kept insolvent institutions in business, and did not clamp down to protect itself against risk, most managers would try to "grow their way" out of their hole. Some others were bound to elect improvidence. Both choices represented far more attractive activities than picking away at expenses.

At the end of 1982 thrift assets totaled $882 billion. Four years later they had risen to the astounding level of $1.407 trillion, an increase of $525 billion that was shared almost equally by savings and loans and savings banks. The latter's enormous relative asset growth, 255 percent, resulted largely when savings and loans converted their charters (by 1986 the operating distinction between the two types had essentially disappeared). Despite this greatly expanded base, expenses as a share of assets soared from 1.34 percent in 1980 (compared to 1.1 percent in the 1960s) to over 2 percent at the end of 1986. The reported net worth ratio improved slightly, but net worth was surely overstated as a result of dubious RAP and GAAP accounting standards. A better, yet still flawed, measurement of thrift performance was the return on assets. After rising to 0.82 percent in 1978, it had declined to below zero in 1981 and 1982. From then, it again rebounded, but only to a 1980s' high of 0.39 percent in 1985. In 1986 it fell again, to 0.09 percent.

The general economic environment provided no explanation for the low level of thrifts' return on assets since 1982. Especially in 1986, when interest rates declined sharply, when housing starts and home sales reached their highest levels since 1978, when residential refinancing mushroomed, and when GNP growth steadily continued, the climate seemed ideal. It certainly was for the majority of institutions, whose return on assets continued and even accelerated. On average, healthy thrifts, which Bank Board chairman Edwin Gray put at 80 percent of the total, had brought the return on assets just about back to where it was in 1978—0.85 percent. But even within this group there were substantial performance differences. Perhaps half the solvent companies, though they represented less than half of total assets, still struggled to get above water. The other half, disproportionately but by no means entirely composed of large thrifts, showed sharp increases in returns on both assets and net worth in 1985, and even sharper increases in 1986.

If those who experienced losses had been simply the inevitable casualties of an industry forced to reconstitute itself, they would have fallen by the wayside and been forgotten. In the next few years some of the marginal institutions would have succeeded, while others would have joined their unfortunate fellows in the grave. Such has been the course of many industries when changing conditions, exacerbated by cyclical downturns, induce a Darwinian result—adaption, extinction, and regeneration. Thrifts, however, are not just another industry in transition. The government, which has minimum net worth to shield its exposure, has guaranteed full payment to their principal creditors, depositors. Had the losses of unsuccessful firms since 1982 been modest and net worth ratios increased substantially, this industry peculiarity would not have mattered. But several hundred already insolvent thrifts managed—and still manage—to lose money by the scores of billions of dollars. A great many more associations, technically solvent, threaten to go into the red. Those losses belong to FSLIC.

Pratt had warned that risk was shifting from mismatched interest rates to ill-chosen assets, but he ignored his own words. While regulators' and academics' attention remained riveted on maturity restructuring and utilization of new asset powers, mainly consumer lending and direct investments, thrifts, many of them recently founded or under new ownership, played an old game. In the 1960s California savings and loans had discovered how to boost earnings by making ADC loans, especially for apartments, for which they could charge high interest rates and fees. Since the loans were short-term, the fees generated far more profits than long-term home loans. Furthermore, the interest rate on such lending could be indexed to the prime rate and adjusted monthly. When not enough takers showed up, partly because developers were insufficiently aggressive or because banks got the business by charging less, association executives initiated projects themselves. However, this constituted direct investing, for which no fees or interest could be booked until construction was completed and sales closed. Californians had solved this problem long ago by creating "disguised" loans; in the 1980s thrift managers adapted and greatly expanded on the practices invented twenty years earlier. Old-time California operators, who had invented such profit-pumping, now clothed themselves in the garb of elder statesmen and condemned these new players.

As in the 1960s (until 1966), when Californians paid a premium for deposits, savings and loans could now raise unlimited funds by paying the price necessary to attract savings; the only precondition was maintenance of a 3 percent net worth ratio to satisfy FSLIC. Furthermore, earnings growth was necessary to accomplish the purpose of virtually all the new or newly acquired stock companies—to operate for a few years and cash in by merging or selling shares to the public. If the economy held up and interest rates stabilized or, preferably, went down, a going charter with a strong earnings record could be sold. What happened after that would not matter. Owners, and even some managers of mutuals, financed virtually any project anywhere as long as the fees and rates were high enough. By lending not only all the development costs but also enough extra funds to cover interest for several years as well as the fees, thrifts could create a self-fulfilling prophecy by booking the interest and fees as current profit. Since nothing in GAAP specifically prohibited such a practice—although auditors are always supposed to look beneath the surface for substance—auditors would go along with it until the completely uneconomic character of the projects was demonstrated.

As early as 1981, owners and operators began capitalizing not just on the new federal legislation but also on changes in state laws and in the regulatory environment. For example, construction lending by all FSLIC-insured associations almost doubled, from $23 billion in 1979 to $43 billion in 1984. Most of this activity was in California, Florida, and Texas, for three reasons: (1) state regulations were lenient; (2) they were the nation's fastest-growing markets; and (3) they had almost 40 percent of the country's total savings and loan assets. In California and Florida, total lending generally followed the pattern of the economy, falling from 1979 to 1982 and rebounding strongly thereafter. In Texas total lending did not change from 1979 through 1981; then it experienced sharp growth through 1985.

The pattern of construction lending and the part of it allocated to a newly authorized property type, commercial real estate, varied markedly among the states. Whereas at no time in California did construction lending reach 25 percent of the total, in Texas and Florida from 1979 through 1981 it was about 30 percent and 40 percent, respectively. The Florida percentage remained at about the same level in 1982 and 1983 and then fell gradually. But Texas was a special case. Total lending there rose 50 percent from 1981 to 1982, and doubled in 1983, to $20 billion. More than half this increase in the crucial years 1982 and 1983 was in construction loans, which had risen nearly six times in Texas, from $1.8 billion in 1978, a prosperous year, to $10.3 billion in 1983. At a time when the state's savings and loans had slightly less in assets than associations in Florida and one-third those in California, they had become the nation's leader in thrift construction lending, with almost double the amount in California and triple the amount in Florida.

Until 1980 savings and loan construction lending was predominantly on residential properties—over 90 percent of the total in 1979, for example. In 1981 the non-residential share of construction lending began to climb, reaching $16.4 billion by 1984, eight times the 1979 level and almost 40 percent of all construction lending. Texas, Florida, and California combined accounted for 75 percent of this new activity.

Obviously, even if such a dramatic rise in risky lending reflected itself in serious losses, the appearance of those losses would lag for two reasons. First, only a borrower's failure to complete construction and ultimate sale at a loss ordinarily forced institutions to book a negative result. Second, thrift managers were sure to defer reporting the bad news as long as possible. Both foreclosure and scheduled-item (troubled loans) ratios rose between 1980 and 1982, the former from 0.13 to 0.33 percent, the latter from 0.80 to 2.62 percent. However, these signs of adversity were attributable largely to the recession. When it ended, then, the ratios should have declined. Instead they soared, the foreclosure ratio to 0.41 percent in 1983 and 1.63 percent in 1986 and the scheduled-item ratio to 0.80 percent in the second half of 1985 and 1.20 percent in 1986.

Thus the emerging evidence showed that lending practices were actually causing harm to many associations, some as early as 1983. It is no surprise that the impact was geographically concentrated in California, Florida, and especially Texas. Write-offs on bad loans and association failures were the principal cause of the overall earnings decline from 1985 to 1986. In 1981–1982 the highest savings and loan losses had come in the New York, Indianapolis, Chicago, and Des Moines districts; in 1986, however, three of these areas, New York, Chicago, and Indianapolis, along with Boston, showed the best return on assets. California's, meanwhile, had fallen to zero in 1984, a result of the failure of a few associations and an enormous loss reported by Financial Corporation of America (FCA; see below). Yet in 1986 most of the state's savings and loans, including virtually all the giants but FCA, showed strong earnings growth, up even from already successful 1985. The return on assets of all California associations, 0.39 percent, however, was the same in 1986 as for the nation in 1985, having been held down by a continuing series of losses in a few institutions. Total disaster came in Texas, where savings and loans lost 2.58 percent of total assets. In California, general economic growth had cushioned the effects of lending improvidence on thrifts as a whole, although many individual institutions suffered badly; in Texas, however, the damaged economy laid bare investment strategies that even prosperity could not have entirely cloaked.

The Regulators

Some savings banks had to be assisted by FDIC, but there is no evidence that these institutions foisted new default obligations on their insurer after 1982. Associations that switched allegiance from FSLIC to FDIC had sufficient net worth and an operating style to protect FDIC. Furthermore, its resources, although small in relation to total assets insured, were far greater than those of its poor sister. If FDIC is in trouble—and it may well be—it is because commercial banks have too little net worth and too many bad loans on construction projects and to foreigners and weak corporations.

By the end of 1986 FSLIC was broke. Lacking the money to liquidate even the worst associations, it had managed to impose a 0.125 percent additional fee on its members—which amounted to a tax on the shareholders of healthy associations, many of whom threatened to escape to FDIC (although few had the required net worth ratio). In the meantime, several hundred insolvent savings and loans were kept alive by deposit insurance, which the public accepted partly because of a 1982 congressional resolution pledging full government support. If the Treasury would in fact honor FSLIC commitments—which, despite the resolution, it is not legally bound to do—the pit would become bottomless. How much more damage, in addition to obligations the agency had already incurred, was built in by bad loans on the books? Worse yet, thousands of managers with everything to gain and nothing to lose were taking new fliers every day.

From 1983 through 1985, while it still could pay the bill, FSLIC liquidated 25 associations, assisted 160 mergers, put 25 institutions under new management (Management Consignment Program, all in 1985), supervised 256 mergers, and approved 542 voluntary mergers. It had also lost members to FDIC. Thus, despite additions by issuance of new charters when the state insurance funds in Ohio and Maryland collapsed, FSLIC membership fell further, from 3,343 in 1982 to 3,247 in 1986. Insured deposits, however, rose from $568 billion to $750 billion.

According to the Bank Board, FSLIC had a net income of $494,000 in 1985 and a $3.9 billion net loss in 1986. Dismal as these results were, FSLIC reported that it still had $3.6 billion in reserves. In May 1987, however, the General Accounting Office (GAO) gave Congress a very different and direr summary of FSLIC's condition: losses of $1.1 billion in 1985 and $10.9 billion in 1986, creating $6.3 billion in negative reserves. The losses would have been even worse without $2.1 billion in income from the special 0.125 percent assessment. Apparently FSLIC was practicing the same kind of accounting legerdemain as its constituent associations. GAO ominously announced that the worst was yet to come:

> The 1986 loss provision is not a projection of the cost of resolving all future problems in the industry. The Corporation [FSLIC] estimates that more than 380 institutions, including the 183 institutions in its current caseload, will ultimately require assistance. The Corporation believes the cost of providing assistance to about 280 currently insolvent institutions may range up to $21 billion. Assistance to another 100 institutions that currently appear to have little chance of recovery could add $4 billion to the Corporation's losses. Future losses cannot be precisely estimated because of various uncertainties, such as the quality of each troubled institution's assets, future levels of interest rates, and the economic outlook for sectors of the economy in which a large portion of the troubled institutions operate.[3]

"Sectors of the economy" was a reference to the "oil patch," mainly Texas. During 1987 signs were hopeful for those areas as oil prices rose above $20 per barrel. By the end of the year, however, the OPEC cartel broke apart and the price of oil fell sharply. Given these circumstances and the Bank Board's long-established propensity to underestimate its insurance obligations, there is every reason to believe that even GAO was overoptimistic.

After lengthy procrastination, induced both by industry opposition and by the intervention of some senators and representatives, notably Texas representative Jim Wright, Congress finally broke a log jam in 1987 when it authorized the twelve Home Loan banks to raise $10.8 billion for FSLIC to spend over three years. The banks' security is a claim against future FSLIC premiums. As in the case of the special assessment, the industry, which owns the Home Loan banks, had grudgingly agreed to be taxed. Healthy firms were becoming increasingly bitter at the prospect of paying ever-greater sums to regulators unable to meet their obligations. Would an increasing share of their profits, which for other reasons may have peaked in 1986 or 1987, be gobbled up by the FSLIC monster? Those hanging on by their fingernails or blatantly insolvent were equally dismayed by added insurance costs. As complete wards of the state, however, they were in no position to complain.

Three Cases

The most colorful stories about thrift misconduct describe out-and-out theft in which managers and owners

engaged in self-dealing to move money outside the institution and into their pockets. In a few instances they did
not even bother with such diversions; they just walked
off with the cash. Reprehensible though such behavior
was, it did not account for a significant share of association losses. These came from people taking risks and
hyping earnings, perhaps even violating laws by consciously misrepresenting the facts to auditors and regulators and conducting business contrary to the rules.
But their intent and expectation was to produce profits
for their institutions. Tapping the till, they knew, had its
limits. Building a small company into a giant with a
record of rapid growth in assets and earnings promised
fortunes. Moreover, if they succeeded, their errant ways
would probably be lost in the euphoria. It never occurred to them that failure sheds harsh light, as three
case histories demonstrate.

Empire Savings

On March 14, 1984, the Bank Board closed Empire Savings and Loan Association of Mesquite, Texas. The company had increased assets nearly eighteen times, from
$17.3 million to $308.9 million, in less than two years.
One month after the Board's action, Chairman Gray
told the House Committee on Government Operations
that Empire's demise would cost FSLIC $163.8 million,
the largest single loss to that date. In August the House
committee issued a report assessing the regulatory
performance.[4]

The report drew three major conclusions:

1. When Spencer H. Blain, Jr., a prominent savings
    and loan figure in Texas and chairman of Empire

since February 1982, purchased majority control of Empire's stock, he did not file the required change-of-control notice. Bank Board officials soon became aware of the violation but took no immediate action. Finally, six months later, Blain was required to put his stock in trust, although he remained chairman and in "effective control."[5]

2. Second, after mid-1982 Empire "engaged in a series of reckless and possibly fraudulent land investment schemes and unsafe and unsound lending practices."[6] Although Board officials were aware of these practices in early 1983, they did not act: "The FHLBB knew a great deal about Empire's growing morass . . . but it did virtually nothing to enforce its extensive supervisory and regulatory powers until quite late in 1983."[7]

3. Third, the committee described in excruciating detail the Board's main justification for its impotence: that Empire's reported earnings showed compliance with net worth requirements. Agency officials admitted, however, that Empire accomplished this only by casting direct investments as loans in order to book income from fees and interest. After demanding an audit, regulators granted nine extensions and waited over a year to get it. Other excuses were lack of sufficient staff and, incredibly, the coincidence of Empire's misconduct with moving the Board's regional office from Little Rock to Dallas.

The Empire case was only one of many illustrating two crucial regulatory issues. First, although there were several indications of improvidence during Pratt's term of office, the task of dealing with the results and answering media and congressional inquiries fell on his successor. Second, Pratt never claimed that the Bank Board lacked the statutory authority to prevent behavior like Empire's or to stop it when discovered, but Gray did: "The new and additional statutory authority we believe we must have in order to provide the necessary tools to supervisory personnel to deal effectively with the emerging problems we face."[8] The committee, however, categorically rejected Gray's contention: "What was lacking was not an absence of authority or power to act, but a void of will to take forceful and effective measures."[9]

Beverly Hills Savings

Beverly Hills (California) Savings and Loan Association converted from mutual to stock ownership with an $18 million stock offering in 1979, at which time it had $400 million in assets and, including the proceeds of the sale, $35 million in net worth—almost a 10 percent ratio. Earnings had risen respectively from $1.4 million in 1976 to $3 million in 1979. In 1980, however, the company broke even, and then lost $14.6 million in 1981, while assets reached $558 million. Although in 1982 Beverly Hills returned to modest profitability of $2.4 million, assets soared to $822 million. The net worth ratio, at 2.5 percent, was thus below regulatory requirements under GAAP accounting.

On April 24, 1985, the Bank Board took over management of Beverly Hills, whose assets, at almost $3 billion, were three and a half times their level two years earlier. Another House group, the Subcommittee on Energy and Commerce, investigated the affair. Chairman John D. Dingell reported that the Bank Board had put $140 million into the association and summarized anticipated findings:

We expect to hear testimony of high-risk lending and joint venture arrangements, inadequate or non-existent control systems, poor lending procedures, possible conflicts of managers and lawyers, lavish management perks and compensation, a mysterious foreign investor, a hostile management take-over, and some accounting and financial reporting judgments that defy both common sense and accepted accounting theories.[10]

Dingell challenged the claim that the regulators' failure to act sooner and with greater effect stemmed solely from their ignorance: "The most disturbing thing is that all of this happened with the apparent longtime knowledge of internal law firms, and Federal and State regulators. Yet the Beverly Hills managers were permitted to continue their activities unabated."[11]

As in the Empire case, rapid growth and high-risk lending were accompanied by a change in control. At Beverly Hills, however, the existing management was able, though only by fighting rigorously, to forestall until April 1984 a takeover by southern California apartment builder Paul Amir. Its policies and administration, then, were what brought Beverly Hills to its knees. According to Amir, he invested and lost $12 million in a company that was already ruined when he finally gained control. In the fourth quarter of 1983, when Beverly Hills had $1.95 billion in assets, its auditors required write-downs causing an $8.4 million loss. Asked by the minority counsel how someone with his experience could buy such a pig in a poke, Amir replied: "I have two responses, one mine and one my wife's. I will tell you my wife's. Midlife crisis [is] . . . probably cheaper than having a mistress." His reasons were ego and the intensity of the takeover struggle. "I somehow got involved in this fight, and I thought even if there are problems, I can solve them; I can turn it around."[12]

Dennis Fitzpatrick, a Beverly Hills executive since 1972 and its chairman in the 1980s, told the committee that management shared the view underlying deregulation: "We could not survive if we continued to do business in the traditional fashion."[13] He outlined the five components of a plan adopted in late 1982:

1. To raise funds wholesale (through brokers)
2. To become a "full service" real estate financial concern—which meant, in addition to making single-family loans, having 10 percent of assets in construction loans, originating permanent commercial property loans, investing 7 percent in real estate joint ventures, and buying real estate for syndication
3. To match maturities
4. To grow to reduce the significance of the existing low-rate portfolio and to facilitate matching
5. To earn higher fees to offset expected lower spreads

Countering Chairman Dingell, James Cirona, president of the San Francisco Home Loan Bank, defended the Bank Board by placing virtually all the blame on state officials:

Garn–St. Germain tipped the balance of equilibrium between the dual State-Federal thrift system in favor of the Federal Charter and many states reacted. None did so with the fervor of California. Clearly, such new found freedom would require added vigilance by regulators in order to facilitate a smooth transition from the traditional thrift to the nearly structural thrift.

What actually took place, however, was just the opposite. From the end of 1979 until April 1985, when Beverly Hills failed, the number of State-chartered thrifts went from 98 to 166. Their assets went from $63 to 112 billion, almost doubling. The administration and professional staff of the California Department of Savings and Loans went from 119 to 68 in the same period, having reached the low point of 30 in April, 1983.[14]

After describing the conduct that destroyed Beverly Hills, Cirona asserted the Bank Board's limitations: too little staff, overwhelming problems, and statutory restraints. Bank Board chairman Gray reiterated this sentiment, as he had when testifying on Empire. He also cited the irony that current claims of his being too lenient came on the heels of criticism that he had acted "precipitously in dealing with the problems of brokered funds, excessive growth, imprudent ADC loans and direct investments."[15] Gray was referring to a series of regulations the Bank Board promulgated in 1984 and 1985, including (1) higher net worth requirements— 6 percent on asset growth and phasing in 6 percent on all assets; (2) a restriction on the use of brokered funds (challenged and overthrown by the courts); (3) a limitation on direct investments to 10 percent of assets; (4) tightened accounting rules on ADC loans; (5) stricter loan underwriting standards; and (6) a virtual ban on new charters.

Chairman Gray appealed to Congress for more operating funds, expanded regulatory powers, and deposit insurance reform giving the Bank Board leeway to charge a higher premium for riskier activities, a proposal made earlier by Pratt and many academic advocates of deregulation. Gray categorically rejected the possibility that added powers for thrifts might be inherently too risky or even that they should not have been implemented until and unless higher net worth requirements were met and the structure of deposit insurance was substantially altered. He said: "I believe that the limited expansion of investment authority in the Garn–St. Germain Act has provided the additional elbowroom which thrifts badly needed to restructure their asset-liability maturing portfolio and to strengthen support for their basic home financing role in the new competitive climate of the 1980s." [16]

Financial Corporation of America

What Gray called "elbowroom" seemed in the cases of Empire and Beverly Hills to be more like an eight-lane highway on which savings and loan managers could import truckloads of money, bought with FSLIC insurance, to invest in high-flying deals, losing not only their modest investments but vast additional sums as well, which would ultimately be paid by either healthy thrifts, the federal government, or both. The way these two firms did business and the trouble they got into were by no means unique: their story was repeated hundreds of times, especially in California and Texas. In a 1987 series of articles entitled "Savings and Looting," one newspaper cited eight companies, in addition to Beverly Hills, in Orange County, California, alone that had been founded since 1980 and later "seized" by FSLIC. What the *Register* called an "epidemic" had created a "$2 billion repair bill" for the agency.[17] In some respects the conduct of these and other associations made that of Beverly Hills and Empire seem tame by comparison. But in the sheer magnitude of his gamble, one man, Charles Knapp, orchestrating one company, Financial Corporation of America, dwarfed all the rest.

Knapp, a former San Francisco investment banker, invested in and took effective control of FCA in the mid-1970s. Although the company owned a small bank (subsequently sold), its main operating vehicle was State Savings and Loan, based in Stockton, California, a small agricultural trading center in the Central Valley. Having grown steadily but still of modest size, with $730 million in assets in 1977, State's main activities were in Stockton and other valley cities. Soon, however, it also opened branches in the major coastal areas, especially in southern California. Knapp drove growth not just in single-family but also in apartment and other real estate lending, doubling assets from 1975 to 1977 and again from 1977 to 1980. Net income tripled.

On the face of it, Knapp was one of the top thrift performers in the country, perhaps the best. Despite State's rapid asset growth, contrary to the industry pattern its net worth ratio did not fall. Rather, from 1977 to 1979 return on net worth rose sharply, from 18.3 percent to 27 percent. And in 1980, when thrift earnings generally dove, State's did not; again it increased return on net worth, to 30 percent, partly because expenses as a percentage of assets were cut dramatically, from 2 percent to 1.5 percent. But it was in the next two years that Knapp apparently demonstrated just how successful a company State was. In 1981 and 1982, when virtually all associations were losing money and many were even shrinking assets, State continued and even increased its rate of growth and earnings. From 1980 to 1982 assets rose three and a half times, from $1.6 billion to $5.7 billion. Though profit increases did not quite keep up, they were still spectacular, rising from $12.4 million in 1980 to $27.3 million in 1982. Return on net worth was 30 percent and 27 percent respectively in the two years. And expenses as a share of assets fell to 1.0 percent in 1981, though they rose to 1.4 percent in 1982.

Knapp was not at all reticent about how he operated. Article after published article contained quotes explaining what he was up to and why he succeeded, as well as depictions of the flashy life-style he led with his glamorous wife, a pilot and owner of an air-chartering service. State, Knapp explained, kept expenses down by buying many of its deposits wholesale—that is, through money desks, not branching. Unlike other companies, State did this mostly with its own sales force rather than through brokers. In fact, $4.9 million of the profits in 1982 came from selling branches as Knapp reduced their importance to the firm's operation.

The other key to State's success, he claimed, was high loan fees and profits on loan sales, originated in-house or purchased from others. Knapp, the former investment banker, had discovered an avenue opened by liability deregulation in the 1980 act: he could now raise unlimited funds and become a trader in mortgages or mortgage-backed securities. This was a pure gamble on interest rates. Wall Street firms, of course, traded all kinds of debt instruments regularly, but they could not, like savings and loans, use a government guarantee (that is, deposit insurance) to borrow thirty times their capital for such a purpose. Knapp's timing was impeccable.

When interest rates skyrocketed in 1980 and again in 1981, State's loan purchases did too, from $42.1 million in 1979 to $198.5 million in 1980, and to $593.2 million in 1982. As rates fell, loans were sold. Profits from the resale of these loans were 33 percent of State's net income in 1980, 25 percent in 1981, and an astounding 100 percent in 1982. In other words, without its mortgage-trading operation the company would have shown no profit in 1982.

Had Knapp run a traditional, single-family, fixed-rate loan operation and used his money-raising organization to fund both these and mortgage purchases, State would have continued to prosper in 1983, been hurt in 1984 by the interest rate spike, and then done very well until early 1987. Overall the results would have been very favorable, especially if he had concentrated on further reductions in operating costs. But his ambitions went far beyond such a strategy. Knapp recognized what other Californians had seen twenty years earlier—that there was a lot of money to be made bidding for deposits and lending the proceeds on ADC loans to generate high fees and interest. He was an extraordinarily skilled trader, but he was an incompetent manager of a major high-risk lending operation. Nor did general economic trends work in his favor. Although the economy in California was hurt less by the 1981–1982 recession and recovered better than the nation as a whole, its agricultural sector, in which much of State's ADC loans were made, suffered. Beyond this, while inflation continued, its rate fell. Knapp was one of a generation of lenders who, for the first time since the early 1960s, would not be bailed out by sharply rising inflation.

State's emphasis on ADC lending was apparent as

early as 1980. While total lending rose 45 percent from 1979 to 1980, construction lending went up 500 percent, nonresidential loans 250 percent, and land loans 300 percent. In the next two years total lending increased 350 percent, with non-single-family loans increasing more than 400 percent. As a result, fee income shot up to $16.3 million in 1980 and almost equaled net income. In 1981 fee income increased 400 percent to $65 million; it reached $88 million in 1982. Clearly fee income, mainly on ADC loans, and gains on loan sales were the keys to FCA's reported profits. Trading, at least as Knapp practiced it in the 1980s, was his own special game. Many others engaged in ADC lending. Knapp simply raised the stakes.

State's success was evident in its published financial statements and was one of the main topics of conversation in virtually every gathering of California industry executives after late 1982. The traditionalists, some of whom had once played Knapp's game, though not with such flair and bravado, condemned him and shared juicy anecdotes demonstrating State's improvidence. By early 1983 a regulator uninformed about Knapp's meteoric and flamboyant rise was peculiarly insulated from reality. Yet when asked in a 1987 interview what he had thought about FCA in early 1983, Pratt denied having heard about the company's conduct during his tenure as Bank Board chairman. Within a few months after Pratt's departure, however, the Bank Board realized that a major problem had developed.

Pratt's successor could not claim ignorance. He was made aware of Knapp's misbehavior by industry executives, if not by Bank Board examiners. More and more evidence showed that State's management had used desperate cover-up measures as their ADC loans had gone bad. Regulators were confronted with another Empire or Beverly Hills, but on a far greater scale. Complicating their dilemma, Knapp came up with a scheme to solve his and the Bank Board's problem: he proposed that State be merged with one of California's premier institutions, American Savings, which had abandoned its freewheeling style of the 1960s and achieved high respectability. Each company had about $10 billion in assets, but American's $700 million net worth was based on a solid, largely single-family, fixed-rate loan portfolio, whose value was rising as interest rates fell. For Knapp it was the ultimate trading gamble on further rate decline. But would he continue risky ADC lending, and would State's existing loans overwhelm the new company with losses?

The proposed merger of two holding companies, First Charter and FCA, provided for a cash payment to be made to Mark Taper, First Charter's founder and major stockholder, for stock to be given to the other First Charter shareholders, and for FCA to be the surviving entity. Knapp would thus be in effective control of one of the largest thrifts in the country. The worrisome possibility for the Bank Board to consider was whether he would then bring down not only State but American along with it, thereby magnifying FSLIC's exposure. Prudence seemed to dictate clamping down on Knapp and denying the application. On August 5, 1983, however, the Bank Board approved it and the merger was consummated. FCA now had over $20 billion in assets, which by September 1984 climbed to $31 billion. In 1985 the Securities and Exchange Commission (SEC) ordered a restatement of FCA's previous earnings. The results of recalculation were a $590 million loss, the largest in thrift history, and a run. The Bank Board forced Knapp to resign, although it did not take formal control of the company. FCA stumbled along with a reported net worth of about 1 percent of assets. In quarter after quarter it announced increases in write-offs for bad loans. After showing modest earnings in 1985 and 1986, $53 million and $95 million respectively, FCA once again went in the red in 1987. Amazingly, while FCA was effectively in receivership in 1985 and 1986, its assets rose by almost $7 billion. The Bank Board anxiously sought a buyer, to whom assistance would, of course, have to be given. Liquidation it deemed prohibitively expensive.

Conclusion

Pratt had clearly identified the risks inherent in thrift deregulation in late 1982 and early 1983 without realizing how much had already gone wrong. He might otherwise have shepherded the process quite differently, phasing it in gradually. Maturity matching required not only lifting liability restrictions but also acclimating to variable-rate loans, a new and complicated way to balance risk. With banks, insurance companies, pension funds, REITs, and investment bankers all pouring money into commercial real estate, a field in which thrifts had no expertise, surely there was no overriding public purpose in adding another source. What was the rush, when thrifts' management skill was extremely limited, their net worth was low and going lower, operating costs were rising, assets were climbing, securitization was serving a growing share of home financing needs, savers had wide choices in depositing their money, and Bank Board funds were inadequate for, and its staff overwhelmed by, existing problems? Why was it desirable to open the floodgates for existing institutions when the risks, as Pratt had acknowledged, were so great and the potential societal benefits so meager? It is even harder to understand what was to be gained by promoting changes of association control and formation of new associations, which were sure to attract imprudent players.

So Pratt rolled the dice, along with Knapp and all the other gamblers. Much of the improvident lending and investment that came due after 1982 was therefore in place or in process when Gray took over the Bank Board. Of equal importance, Pratt had convinced key members of Congress that all was going well, as Gray's Senate confirmation hearings reflected. Garn and his Senate committee colleagues expressed only two concerns: would thrifts stop making home loans, and would they become commercial banks? Gray told the senators not to worry and showered praise on Garn and Pratt for having so wisely legislated deregulation. No one asked the new Bank Board chairman about risky loans. If he had read the admonitions in *Agenda for Reform*, they apparently did not register. Not until late 1983 did Gray demonstrate any concern about investment quality. In speech after speech he hammered away at one issue—the need to make ARMs.

Most thrift failures since 1982 had the same elements: (1) extensive ADC lending, much of it disguised direct investment; (2) a new charter or a change of control; (3) rapid growth, often funded by brokered deposits; and (4) the booking of high fees. Despite direct investments' being falsely classified as loans, in many instances they too rose dramatically. Like Knapp, some operators also played the money market by originating or purchasing fixed-rate loans for resale without hedging or arranging commitments at a price; when rates spiked in 1984, briefly in 1986, and again in 1987, they were badly hurt.

By early 1984 Gray finally understood that ADC lending and direct investments were whirling out of control, especially in Texas, California, and Florida. His initial response was to propose a regulation curtailing brokered deposits. Bitterly opposed by investment bankers, many savings and loan executives, administration officials, notably Donald Regan, and some members of Congress, Gray nevertheless got a watered-down rule. But it was successfully challenged in the courts. In the next three years he issued statement after statement to Congress and the industry, warning of the dire consequences of rapid growth, minimal capital, and improvident investments. At one point, a key member of Congress told him to stop pushing so hard for reregulation. In 1985, Regan, now White House chief of staff, suggested that Gray resign because there was too much turmoil in the industry. Members of Congress, especially those from affected areas, urged forbearance. When Gray sought money to add examiners and increase their pay, added powers to restrain thrift conduct, and funds to close insolvent associations, he was chastised by the White House and rebuffed by Congress. He did manage to get the Bank Board to impose stricter accounting rules and capital requirements, as well as limitations on direct investments.

Three concerns drove the enactment of deregulatory

statutes and their liberal administration. First was the savers' increasing clamor for full access to market interest rates. Second was a presumed housing crisis in which the gap between demographic need and actual production would be widened by restricted mortgage fund availability. Third was the bleak condition of thrifts, which not only contributed to the shrinking mortgage supply but threatened to bankrupt FSLIC. In reality, residential production snapped back strongly after 1982; vacancies and surpluses replaced shortages as household formations tailed off, and the country was awash with mortgage money. The problem for thrifts seemed more and more to be a shortage not of funds but of safe investments at decent spreads.

The squeeze on the profits of even healthy thrifts, as well as the continuing deterioration of those near insolvency, began to show up dramatically in late 1987 and early 1988. The industry showed losses of $3.2 billion in the fourth quarter of 1987; they rose to $3.9 billion in the first quarter of 1988 and fell only slightly in the second quarter, to $3.6 billion. News accounts attributed these results entirely to write-downs of bad loans. This certainly occurred; weak institutions typically continued as long as possible to understate asset devaluation and thus present an overpositive portrait of their financial condition. Even worse, however, was a sharp drop in earnings for the solvent associations caused by accounting reforms, by a rise in the cost of funds, by the cost of supporting FSLIC, and by the persistent reduction in income caused by the use of teaser interest rates on ARM loans. At conference after conference, savings and loan executives flagellated themselves and their colleagues for paying too much for deposits (at least 60 basis points more than banks) and giving borrowers a gift of first-year loan interest at or below 7 percent, and thus at or below cost. Nevertheless, there was no evidence that thrifts would make the required adjustment by limiting liability growth, or even shrinking liabilities to induce a reduction in deposit interest rates and a rise in ARM home loan yields, and by driving operating costs down commensurately.

Had inflation and interest rates skyrocketed and the economy faltered after 1982, the already precarious situation could have become virtually impossible to control. Fate, however, gave Pratt and his successors six years of economic growth and low interest rates. Although blessed with such good fortune, they made matters far worse than they found them. As bad as recent financial reports have been, savings and loans are far worse off than their accounting indicates. What remains of this story involves finding the answers to three questions: Could government officials have avoided the debacle? If so, why did they err so badly? What happens next?

7

Assessment

What Should Have Been Done

As early as the 1970s, the Bank Board should have pushed associations harder toward variable-rate lending. It was hampered by strong resistance from Congress on one side and thrift executives on the other. The former, in fact, warned the Bank Board in 1977 not to embrace ARMs. But Jay Janis, Pratt's immediate predecessor, authorized them anyway. Deregulation of liabilities began when the ceiling on large-denomination certificates of deposit was lifted in 1973. It was advanced by the New England experiment initiated in 1974, by money market certificates in 1978, and, of course, by the 1980 act. It was virtually completed by 1982, when thrift money market accounts were authorized, although the final step, removal of passbook-rate ceilings, did not come until 1986.

Deregulation accomplished two basic and necessary purposes: (1) savers were given improved services and rates, and (2) thrifts could compete for funds. It was on the asset side that major change was neither needed nor wise, since thrift management had no expertise in commercial real estate lending and since the field was full of active participants. The only justification, if any, for permitting thrifts to engage in such lending lay with small-property loans, with which others might not bother. Allowing 20 percent (1980) and then 40 percent (1982) of assets for commercial real estate lending was hardly necessary to facilitate entry into this tiny niche. Similarly, consumer lending might be useful on a spot basis, and in fact thrifts have increased such lending modestly—to about 2 percent of assets in 1987.

Enhancing the direct-investment authority was foolhardy. By 1980 federally chartered institutions had already gotten themselves into trouble in one area by undertaking development projects. In Chicago, for example, home production and sales rebounded strongly after the 1973–1975 recession. Many savings and loans there, primarily mutuals, created service companies and used them to buy land for joint ventures with local builders. When the Chicago housing market turned down in the late 1970s, showing weakness as early as 1978, several associations found themselves owning land, site improvements, and even houses for which there was little or no demand. Their joint-venture partners, who had put up no money, simply walked away. Although negative portfolio spreads were a more serious and dramatic problem in the early 1980s, a number of Illinois associations suffered losses from direct investments well after 1982.

While legislatively expanded asset powers contributed to the thrift debacle, the main culprit was implementation. The Bank Board's fundamental mistake was not conditioning both growth and riskier investment on higher net worth ratios. Furthermore, it should have declared an absolute moratorium on new charters, state or federal, on the grounds that it did not have the financial or supervisory resources to deal with associations already in existence. Acquisition of existing charters should have been allowed only when sufficient new capital and improved management would be introduced to reduce the agency's exposure. The kinds of investment and accounting games played by Empire, Beverly Hills, FCA, and many others were inevitable unless regulators stopped them. The Bank Board should have promulgated its own accounting rules, even if they were stricter than GAAP, and established an early watch program for rapidly growing associations, especially those emphasizing ADC loans and fee income.

There were two opposing approaches to revitalizing the thrift industry in the 1980s. Under one, after the inevitable recession the Fed would succeed in getting inflation under control; then housing production and sales, as well as the general economy, would rebound. To be precise about timing or interest rates was not necessary; thrifts could restructure their portfolios gradually. How much each built its net worth ratio would depend on three factors: (1) the capability with which it managed its business, especially by controlling costs and containing asset losses; (2) the degree of competition from securitization; and (3) the conduct of other thrifts. Only so many safe loans were available, and only so many dollars could be attracted at given spreads. To grow, thrifts had to bid the cost of money up and its yield down, reducing gross interest spreads. Net profit would be driven even lower by rising expenses; pretax return on assets and net worth ratios would therefore decline. The solution to this competitive squeeze was obvious: to limit not only the number of thrifts but their total assets as well. The surviving institutions would then be able to achieve high enough net spreads to earn and attract capital. As an insurer, FSLIC had every motive to promote such an outcome.

This approach to the plight of thrifts took into account the possibility, if not probability, of the economic events that actually unfolded; it was not based on the existence of a housing crisis or supportive of diversification and high-risk investments, and it sought to facilitate maturities matching. Its objective was to protect FSLIC by raising net worth ratios, even if that meant containing asset growth. Of course, ADC loans, direct investments, consumer lending, junk bond buying, and any number of other activities might increase earnings, but they were just as likely, if not more likely, to generate losses. Pratt himself had made this clear in *Agenda for Reform.*

The Bank Board chose the second, opposite, approach: it encouraged changes of control and new charters, interpreted existing rules as liberally as possible, kept insolvent thrifts afloat, and fostered asset growth. It ignored the signs of improvidence found in its own reports, including the burst of ADC lending in California, Florida, and especially Texas; the rising proportion of those loans on commercial properties; earnings heavily dependent on fee income; and asset growth rates that were virtually impossible to obtain without sacrificing credit quality. When Gray realized what was going on, he proposed some constructive actions. Mild as these actions were, they were bitterly opposed by much of the industry, many members of Congress, the White House, and his colleagues on the Bank Board. Gray asked for far less change in direction than was required, but he was still forced to compromise.

Justifications

Three main justifications have been given for the thrift debacle, none of which stand up to scrutiny.

> 1. The interest rate and housing scenario that actually happened could not have been predicted or even conceived.

Cyclicity has been a feature of the U.S. economy for over 150 years. Housing production and interest rates have moved consistently in quite long swings. Why was it axiomatic that inflation would not be brought under control and home building would not rebound? In fact, my conclusion to a history of large-scale home building after the war, written in 1981, predicted the trends on inflation and interest rates:

> [Since] reduction of inflation is of transcendent importance, almost certainly then the 1980s will be different not only from the 1970s but the entire period since World War II. . . . For example, mortgage interest rates would go down but only as the anticipated inflation rate also declines. While the rate of inflation is falling, presumably a period of several years, the real interest rate will be at least 3 percent, and possibly more.[1]

On lender behavior:

> Lenders will demand variability to protect them against later reversals of the inflation trend. . . .

Savings and loans now losing money will need at least this spread to make a profit. They are likely to seek even more to offset the low rates on their existing portfolios.[2]

On housing production:

In 1981 housing starts will almost certainly be at or below 1980. In 1982 and 1983 starts might increase modestly to about 1.3 million and 1.4 million respectively, compared to 1.5 million in 1976 and 2 million in 1977. The following year, 1984, might show a further rise but would be well below 1978.[3]

In most respects I was overpessimistic. Mortgage rates and inflation fell more rapidly and further and housing starts rose higher than I predicted. I underestimated the severity of the 1981–1982 recession but also the strength of the recovery. Nevertheless, the basic trends suggested were correct.

In 1982 I had a long discussion with Pratt and Beesely. I argued vehemently for the restriction of new charters, ADC lending, direct investments, and asset growth. I described the California and Illinois ADC lending experiences, not to mention the REIT problems of the 1970s, contending that there would be similar or worse results if thrifts were driven into new asset activities with which they had no experience and which other institutions were conducting. I illustrated my point with a true anecdote. Recently, I had asked a Florida thrift executive what kind of lending he expected to undertake in the new regulatory environment. He had replied: "I will never make another loan; the government lets me sell T[reasury] bills and do what I want with the money.

This is the greatest venture capital opportunity ever seen. I am going to do deals, mostly in real estate." How many thrift managers, I asked Pratt and Beesely, could be given such authority without FSLIC being buried? And would granting new charters not make matters worse? Pratt and Beesely did not deny the risks. Indeed, Beesely seemed genuinely concerned. Pratt, however, was unmoved.

2. Officials could not have known about dangerous investment practices until it was too late to act.

The Bank Board receives regular financial reports from individual associations and assembles data in research reports. Had Pratt instructed his subordinates to identify signs of imprudent conduct—rapid asset growth, rising percentages of ADC lending and fee income, sudden bursts of direct investment—by individual companies or in geographic areas, he could have concentrated examination and supervisory resources where they were needed. At every industry gathering he and his top staff could also have held informal meetings to elicit off-the-record opinions on emerging credit problems. If Pratt became aware of the potential danger only late in his term, he should then have made sure his successors and Congress understood the warnings contained in his December 1982 speech and in *Agenda for Reform*. There is no indication he did so. Bank Board reports showing a sharp rise in ADC lending, including its emphasis in Texas on commercial property, were available to Gray if he chose to read them. He did not. Thus, it was not a lack of evidence but failure to pay attention to it that accounts for Pratt's and, initially, Gray's ignorance.

3. The Bank Board lacked funds, experienced staff, and authority to handle the situation.

If Pratt had really felt inhibited, his record would, like Gray's, contain a series of rejected appeals to Congress. Yet he made no such appeals. Of course, there is bound to be disagreement about how far either could have gone. Gray claims that budgeting and statutory restraints were crucial impediments to action after the danger was finally perceived. Jay Janis disagrees. Although we cannot know if Janis is right, it is clear that Pratt never tried either to use existing authority to restrain improvident thrift conduct or to gain more power and money from Congress.

Explanation and Blame

I have now come to the most difficult and, to me at least, the most important part of this study—explaining why the government created the thrift debacle and assigning blame. If, as I have tried to show, the only way to rebuild savings and loan net worth ratios and profitability was to shrink their number and assets in accordance with the reduced need for them to originate or hold portfolio home loans, why was the opposite done? And why, when there was already a glut of institutions and mechanisms to provide other types of financing, were thrifts not just allowed but virtually driven into high-risk lending and even into undertaking exotic ventures on their own account? Was the cause official venality? Unfortunately, it was not. If it had been, the cost would have been far less, and the entertainment value far greater. Instead we must look for our understanding to a confluence of ideology, personality, and circumstance.

The ideology was deregulation, a belief that virtually all the economic ills that became evident in the 1970s— inflation, lower productivity, the 1973–1975 recession, minimal GNP growth, and so forth—were the result of excessive government interference. The proposed counterrevolution, instigated to overthrow Keynesianism, had come to dominate the intellectual debate. Even Democrats joined the chorus of complaint and advocated loosening the heavy public hand. But the most ardent advocates of deregulation were found among conservatives or neoconservatives, the latter evidencing the typical ardor of converts. Their political hero was Ronald Reagan. When he gained the White House, their fondest hopes seemed about to be realized.

The banking system, however, did not lend itself to substantial regulatory change, and for four reasons. First, the process for eliminating controls on deposit interest rates in both banks and thrifts had already been set in motion by the 1980 act. Second, banks, especially large ones, were in deep trouble because of loans to developing countries. Third, Reagan was well aware of the threat posed by major bank failures. Fourth, in the most important position overseeing banking stood Paul Volcker, a man of enormous stature, strong will, and legal and psychological independence. Volcker was concerned about banks' vulnerability and committed to guiding them through a difficult transition. The last thing he wanted to do was encourage them to increase risk.

The thrift situation was quite different. For deregulationists, it presented a perfect example of mistaken government intervention, in this case to promote housing, federal support for which, they believed, had been overdone and should be ended. Thus, the old quid pro quo for savings and loans—that to specialize in residential finance meant getting deposit insurance, tax benefits, powers not available to banks, and a competitive advantage in attracting deposits—should be abandoned. Thrifts, the argument went, should be weaned from the government's teat. If they continued to concentrate on home loans, either by shifting to ARMs or by operating as mortgage bankers, they would have to do so in open competition with banks, nondepository mortgage bankers, or any other players. If they became indistinguishable from banks, the market would determine who would survive. If they were forced out of business, so be it.

Reagan immediately got the opportunity to appoint a new Bank Board chairman. His selection was Richard T. Pratt, avowed deregulator who brought fierce determination, contempt for the industry he was about to supervise, and arrogance to the job. In two years—he made clear his intention to move on after that—Pratt intended to drag savings and loans into the twenty-first century. That many of them would die along the way did not faze him a bit.

Pratt was a protégé of Jake Garn of Utah, who became chairman of the Senate Banking Committee. To head the committee's staff, Garn selected M. Danny Wall, formerly redevelopment director for Salt Lake City. This triumvirate wrote the Garn–St. Germain act of 1982, with Pratt as spearhead, Garn as senior legislator, and Wall as technician. Treasury secretary Regan, another counterrevolutionary, added a compelling voice during legislative hearings. And in the White House, thrift deregulation fell naturally into the lap of Edwin Gray. At fifty-three, almost twenty years older than Pratt, Gray had been a journalist, newscaster, public relations specialist for Pacific Telephone Company, press secretary to Reagan when he was governor of California, and marketing executive for a large San Diego savings and loan. He went to the White House in 1981 to coordinate domestic policy. Gray had neither Pratt's ideological zeal nor his force of personality, but he was familiar with the thrift business and deeply loyal to Reagan.

The president played no role either in designing and advocating the legislation or in determining the Bank Board's management. The details bored him, and his support was not needed. Unlike other administration thrusts—reduced tax rates, lower domestic spending, increased military outlays, and, of course, Contra aid— thrift deregulation faced little opposition on the Hill for three reasons: The dire condition of thrifts made the Congress sympathetic to reform; deregulation had become a widely accepted proposition; and the main thrift trade group, the U.S. League for Savings Associations, had tremendous clout. Not only could Bank Board members not be appointed or legislation passed against the League's opposition, but League staff even drafted many acts and regulatory provisions itself. The League was wary of deregulation and of Pratt. It fought successfully to retain tax advantages for savings and loans and lenience toward its weak members. Of course, it supported giving thrifts investment powers previously denied to them but available to banks, such as consumer and commercial lending, credit card issuance, and commercial real estate loans. And it won for savings and loans an expanded opportunity not attained by banks: direct investment in real estate. The League knew that if Pratt had his way, the special role of thrifts, and therefore of their trade association, would be taken away. But they were able to get much of what their members wanted while retaining the wall separating savings and loans from banks.

Pratt spent virtually his entire two years as Bank Board chairman shepherding the Garn–St. Germain bill through Congress, publicly arguing the case for deregulation, and coping with those associations that were so destitute and obviously mismanaged that they had to be taken over. Pratt knew, and publicly avowed, that granting all these powers to savings and loans which had little or no net worth and allowing hundreds of new entrants into the business was fraught with danger and totally inconsistent with providing federal deposit insurance or with expecting savings and loans to continue specializing in portfolio home lending. When he discovered, however, that Congress and the League would not give up deposit insurance or the traditional thrift role, he plunged ahead anyway. His lack of interest in managing his agency, his deeply held views, and his giant ego impelled him on. He was like a bull who had begun the charge and could not now alter course.

Under family pressure, Gray left Washington, D.C., in August 1982 to return to his home in San Diego and resume a private career as a savings and loan executive. Yet when many thrift and League officials pressured him to take Pratt's place, he agreed. An eminently likeable man, Gray could not refuse the affection and trust offered him by those in the industry or pass up the prestige and the first chance in his life to be a chief executive. His confirmation hearings were a love feast; there was no inkling of the disaster already pending. In each of five separate and lengthy interviews, Gray assured me that he had no idea there were problems "on the asset side." Although this seems incredible in the light of Pratt's repeated warnings and the information contained in agency reports, it is, I believe, true.

When Gray began to understand the implications of investment improvidence, he tackled the issue obliquely by attempting to restrict associations' ability to attract deposits through brokers. This proved ineffective. While deposit brokering often accompanied excessive growth and bad lending, in theory—and sometimes in practice—there was no necessary connection. The Bank Board chairman should immediately have begun telling Congress and the industry that stopping new charters and curbing asset powers were essential to FSLIC's soundness. He did finally do so, but his proposed actions were only partly accepted by fellow board members, Congress, and the League. Thus, his efforts, however laudable, were too little and too late. Gray became a pariah in both camps: To the ideologues he was that worst of all things, a "reregulator"; to those who saw what needed to be done, he was an ineffectual captive of the League and the industry.

Gray's successor, Danny Wall, bears only limited responsibility for the thrift debacle. As a congressional staff member, he helped shape thrift legislation. Later, as Bank Board chairman, he tried to cover up the failure of deregulation until after the next elections—an effort in which, as far as the press is concerned, he has failed. By the middle of 1988 hardly a day passed without a news story characterizing the thrift situation as a disaster and estimating its cost at $50 billion to $100 billion. Wall has doggedly insisted that the bill will be far less and can be borne entirely by the industry. He may have convinced himself, but hardly anyone else.

Bank Board members are supposed to be independent regulators. If this implies independence of thought, none of the three Reagan appointees qualify. All, especially Pratt, were taken in by a gross oversimplification—the idea that all that thrifts needed was the removal of government control. None of them grasped two essential aspects of American history. First, since the early 1800s, high-risk lending, especially on real estate, has destroyed an increasing number of financial institutions at increasingly heavy costs. These failures contributed to, and in turn were caused by, cyclical downturns. Second, the New Deal was a direct reaction to an overwhelming sentiment that the government must prevent a recurrence of depressions, with deposit insurance an integral part of the package. There is no evidence that American voters have become tolerant of the prospect of another 1929–1932. Whatever the theoretical efficacy of abandoning or significantly altering deposit insurance—which is what intellectuals contend ought to be done—there was no practical reason to assume Congress would do so. Even the president has never endorsed such a notion.

In 1981, chairing the Bank Board called for prudence and for intense management. Instead the Bank Board got Pratt, a go-for-broke zealot bored with the day-to-day business of his agency. When he left, the job called for someone with sufficient nerve and stature to tell everyone—the president, Congress, the League, the industry—that the course of deregulation should be reversed and the mess cleared up immediately, at a cost of several billion dollars. Instead the Board got Gray, a man of reasonable intelligence but severely limited scope, who could not initially imagine calamity and who could not convince others of reality when he finally perceived it. When Gray left, the job called for a ruthless and extraordinarily talented workout manager, beholden to no interested party and willing to assign responsibility for the debacle wherever it fell. Instead the Board got Wall, a minor congressional operative.

Pratt, Gray, and Wall all lacked crucially important attributes. None had sufficient sense of history, sufficient strength, sufficient skill, or sufficient independence to carry out a very difficult task successfully. Their fellow Board members, League officials, members of Congress, and, of course, savings and loan managers must share responsibility, as must the intellectuals who gave them all an erroneous and sometimes fraudulent prescription. Curiously, however, Ronald Reagan, who should bear much of the blame, has for eight years remained entirely aloof from the disaster and has received no press attention in connection with it. The thrift debacle is a consequence of regulatory mismanagement during his two terms as president.

Recently, Reagan has been criticized for initiating highly controversial and dangerous policies and abandoning their conduct to overzealous subordinates. Selling arms to Iran is the most noteworthy example. The thrift debacle, the greatest regulatory financial disaster in American history, is Irangate's domestic counterpart. When administering deregulation, however, the executive branch was not acting against the wishes of Congress, as it was in dealing with the Ayatollah. Congress, in fact, was a strong advocate of forbearance toward insolvent associations. It was in no position to play its traditional role of checking presidential mania. As a result, the thrift conflagration has raged out of control, as politicians desperately avoided taking responsibility for its occurrence or for the massive public cost of putting it out. But the history of the thrift debacle must someday place the primary blame where it belongs, on Reagan, an ideological puritan who proclaimed the virtues of deregulation and then left its implementation to men ill equipped to handle such a delicate task. When asked why he did not ever brief Reagan on the severity of the thrift situation, its causes, and the steps required to deal with it, Gray replied that Reagan had had no interest in the matter—he left it to ideologues like Donald Regan and the people at the Office of Management and Budget. In four years as Bank Board chairman, Gray said, he never talked to the president, and it never occurred to him to do so. When he tried to reregulate, not only did the White House not help, but it was his worst enemy.

The Future

The main prerequisite for dealing with the thrift debacle is the same as it was in 1980—an assessment of the situation made without ideological bias or assumptions of either a catastrophic or a prosperous economic environment. Had regulators exercised restraint, there need only have been a minor claim on FSLIC. Now, however, claims could exceed $100 billion. The thrift industry and its insurer constitute a workout problem far greater than Chrysler, Lockheed, Penn Central, or even

New York City. Most of the cost does not derive from the fall in oil prices and the resultant collapse of the oil-patch economies, mainly in Texas. Insurance is supposed to handle just such an event. Had the Bank Board prevented associations from growing so fast and making risky investments, had it paid special attention to evidence of burgeoning ADC lending, FSLIC could have taken the Texas hit in stride. Gray, to his credit, did not blame the Texas losses primarily on the state's economy.

Unfortunately, the nation's economy is not likely to be so kind after 1987 as it was after 1982. Interest rates may fall, but probably not by much. Furthermore, lower interest rates have become a mixed blessing, because they make fixed-rate loans more attractive. Whatever the merits of the idea, removal of agency status from Fannie Mae and Freddie Mac is politically dead. They will continue to offer thrifts competition that gets stiffer as rates come down. Ironically, institutions that now are largely restructured may actually do worse than the others if rates fall.

As already happened in 1987 and is virtually certain to happen in the next few years, the home financing pie is declining in size. The total fell from $460 billion in 1986, the peak year of the 1980s, to $350 billion in 1987. Refinancing was 60 percent lower in the first quarter of 1988 than in the same period in 1987. With securitization competition unalterable, if thrift assets and operating costs continue to rise, not only will spreads be sacrificed, but so will loan quality. Another regional economic downturn, a general recession, or, what may be more probable, reduced GNP growth rates accompanied by minimal inflation will expose the weak credit standards used by many thrifts making ARM loans.

Dual banking is an anachronism. It served Americans well as long as they were willing to accept its negative consequences—namely, failures, depositor losses, and exacerbation of depressions. After 1929–1932 the American public voted for programs designed to prevent depressions and banking collapses. States, which bear no financial risk, should not be allowed to set standards in conflict with those of FSLIC. To have the federal government underpinning depository institutions—in the case of thrifts, only to promote housing—and then to plead for a free market makes no sense. Pratt and his followers have made their case. While Congress rejected their argument, the Bank Board allowed substantial new thrift risk-taking without requiring any additional protection, notably increased capital.

There is still a housing role for thrifts, although it has been relatively and absolutely reduced by demographic changes, securitization, and the success of forty years of high housing production levels. The sine qua non for these institutions (as it is for banks) is to increase net worth ratios while containing risk. Since the demand for their principal product is falling, since even healthy associations are paying at least 0.60 percent more for deposits than banks, since profit margins have been insufficient to raise net worth ratios significantly, and since the industry must bear part of FSLIC obligations, *total assets must be shrunk.* In no other way can thrifts achieve the required gross and net spreads to put themselves and FSLIC back on a sound footing. The industry's capital-to-asset ratio under RAP fell dramatically from March 1987 to March 1988, from 4.54 percent to 3.44 percent, the result of asset growth, losses by insolvent institutions, and a decline in earnings of healthy associations. Under GAAP even the "solvent" savings and loans—those with positive net worth—had only a 2.46 percent ratio. If the Bank Board continues to allow asset growth, effectuates mergers rather than liquidations, and closes only the five hundred or so weakest firms, net worth ratios will fall even further.

At the end of 1988, FSLIC-insured savings and loans will have about $1.3 trillion in assets, more than double the level in 1980, and about $40 billion in net worth, a 3 percent ratio. GAAP-insolvent associations—those with reported negative net worth—number about five hundred and have about $125 billion in assets. Although their book deficit is about $10 billion, savings and loan accounting significantly overstates asset value in four principal ways: (1) goodwill, which represents no physical or marketable value, is carried as an asset; (2) writedowns on bad loans or investments are insufficient; (3) FSLIC paper provided to prop up net worth is booked as an asset; and (4) below-market-interest-rate loans are not discounted. The fourth item might be accepted as tolerable in the current interest-rate environment, but the others should be adjusted to reflect a realistic view of "tangible" or real net worth. Although only the Bank Board has the data and the staff to make such a calculation, doing so would likely show at least five hundred more associations, with at least $175 billion more in assets, to have negative net worth.

If earnings had been rising at a faster rate than assets, net worth ratios would have reversed their decline. But the opposite is the case. For the industry as a whole, earnings peaked in 1985, before the impact of major losses from improvident lending began to hit balance sheets. In 1986 the healthy firms continued to report improved profits. The following year, however, even for those associations, earnings began a decline, which accelerated in 1988. As demand for home financing, especially refinancing, fell and as thrift assets continued to climb, the squeeze on spreads tightened. Even solvent firms found themselves forced to write off loan losses, and, of course, they continued to pay a special premium to FSLIC. In the first quarter of 1988, GAAP-solvent savings and loans earned only 0.30 percent on assets. The most efficient savings and loan will struggle to earn more than 0.50 percent on assets or 10 percent on equity. The twelve largest savings and loans, with $228 billion in assets, showed a decline in return on assets from 0.76 percent to 0.47 percent between the first half of 1987 and the first half of 1988. The industry average, even after merger of the insolvent associations, will be far lower.

In the third quarter of 1988 the Bank Board announced that several insolvent associations in the Southwest had been merged and given substantial FSLIC-paper infusions of capital to make them appear sound. Regulators hoped thus to improve operating efficiency and reduce deposit costs. In other instances the Board had taken over associations and sold them to outsiders. New capital from the sales ranged from 1 to 3 percent of assets, in return for which buyers got four crucial benefits: (1) protection against loss on bad assets; (2) a guaranteed spread on existing assets and liabilities; (3) tax losses to apply against future profits; and (4) the right to borrow from the association for their own projects.

The Board also announced the sale of American Savings, FCA's principal operating subsidiary, to Texas billionaire Robert Bass. The government will provide Bass a $15 billion "good bank"; the bad assets are to be put in a "bad bank" with FSLIC bearing all losses. Bass will put $500 million, or 3.33 percent of assets, into the company. American will be allowed to lend up to $1.5 billion to a merchant bank wholly owned by Bass, in which he will invest only $50 million. In addition, Bass is to get $1 billion in tax cover, which may be applicable to the merchant bank. As in the Southwest transactions, FSLIC will retain a minority interest in future profits.

Despite the avowedly minuscule net worth ratios and the special risk-taking permitted in these and similar transactions, Chairman Wall justifies them on the grounds that liquidation of the insolvent associations would be more costly, estimating the cost differential at 25 percent. He has not given the public or Congress any data to back this claim. On the face of it, his conclusion is wrong for three reasons: first, the tax loss carried forward would disappear under liquidation and the Treasury would therefore benefit; second, under liquidation only insured depositors need to be paid, whereas all creditors are satisfied by restructuring; and third, propping up these institutions keeps the spreads of the rest of the industry under downward pressure. Furthermore, the estimates of outlays for guarantees given to these associations, like virtually all projections made by the Board, are almost certainly optimistic. What will regulators do a few years from now when their "partners" return for more help?

Through September 1988 FSLIC notes and guarantees to restructured savings and loans exceeded $20 billion, almost twice previous estimates. Presumably these outlays, as well as those yet to be committed, are to come from the profits of healthy associations. Members of Congress, however, have begun to doubt that this is possible. They are becoming increasingly aware of the industry's bleak earnings picture, even after discounting losses of insolvent firms, and increasingly skeptical of the Bank Board's projections. The executive branch itself has become wary of Wall's continuing assurances that no public money will be required. The Treasury Department recently announced its intention to conduct an independent study of the matter. Despite congressional concern, few legislators have chosen to do more in an election year than complain that regulators have misinformed them and overstepped their authority. When Wall, responding to legislators' obvious dismay, stares them down and says in effect, "All you have to do to stop me is pass new laws mandating liquidation and appropriating the funds to do it," banking committee members growl but slink back into their cages.

The thrift industry is characterized by such low earnings that unless the Bank Board virtually guarantees future profits, new capital can be attracted only from players who want to throw the dice on very high leverage and risky investments. Managers of at least a thousand associations are already in this position. Prudent conduct cannot possibly achieve the 6 percent net worth ratio the Bank Board has edicted. Only by trying to circumvent the spirit, if not the letter, of growth and investment regulations can they hope to prosper. In pursuing such a course, those who run public companies fulfill their duties to their owners. However improbable success may be, its fruits go to shareholders; the losses go to FSLIC. It is this division of profit and loss that government officials chose in the early 1980s. The regulations have been modified to curb the most flagrant abuses, but the required fundamental change in direction has not been made. Taxing healthy associations, many of which are themselves destitute and most of which are losing ground, to subsidize a few of their number in taking over the operations of those in even worse straits may improve operating efficiency slightly and prevent gross profligacy. This course, in short, may postpone catastrophe, but only by making its ultimate occurrence more likely and its potential severity greater.

Danny Wall and his colleagues on the Bank Board desperately delude themselves with a Panglossian prediction: "Somehow it will all work out." Having been intimately involved with the creation of the thrift debacle, they cannot bring themselves to tell the president, Congress, and the citizenry that they made a dreadful error, which will probably cost $50 billion to $100 billion or more to correct. Clearly an industry with $50 billion in book net worth, much of it specious, and with a continuing decline of earnings cannot pay this bill. The taxpayer must pay most of it. Yet if government leaders are unwilling to face up now to such a cost, some of which the industry can pay, why should depositors retain confidence a few years hence when a recession, a regional shock, an interest rate spike, or a combination thereof drives the potential outlay to several hundred billion dollars and when most savings and loans are effectively bankrupt? At that point, assurances of depositer safety will rightly be seen as empty utterances. Then the run that regulators have so long feared will begin. After Wall assumed his new post, he said that those expecting elected representatives to appropriate vast sums to pay for the Bank Board's mismanagement would be disappointed. He may be right, but his is a truly pessimistic view of American democracy. Continuing on the present course, allowing the wish to avoid taxpayer responsibility to become father to the thought, is a ticket to certain disaster.

If lucky enough to have continued economic growth and price and interest rate stability, the next president can offer a program to take the losses now before the situation is truly unmanageable. Its main components would be as follows:

1. To apply accounting principles that more accurately measure tangible net worth
2. To schedule the five-year phasing-in of a minimum tangible net worth requirement
3. To immediately close and liquidate every association with a current deficit, unless a buyer meets the net worth requirement by injecting funds from outside the industry
4. To prevent asset growth and ADC lending or direct investments by associations not meeting the minimum net worth requirement and to limit their character and amount even for those that do
5. To continue to close and liquidate associations when they clearly cannot meet the minimum net worth requirement either through earnings or by raising outside capital

If this program is adopted, about a thousand savings and loans, with about $300 billion in assets, will be closed almost immediately and most will be liquidated. Several hundred more will probably disappear over the next five years. The number of associations and their assets may continue to shrink thereafter, if securitization of fixed-rate home loans expands its market share (it has fallen recently as ARMs have become more popular) or if it comes to dominate variable-rate lending. In any event, the scale of the thrift industry should find whatever level will maintain sufficient net worth to protect FSLIC and provide a reasonable return on equity. Earnings will come, and should continue to come, from origination of home loans, for portfolio or resale, and from ancillary activities. If, as many analysts believe, such a posture would lead to the ultimate demise of most, if not all, savings and loans, so be it. This would mean that the market demand for residential financing is being efficiently met by securitization and nonthrift mortgage banking. If the government decides to foster housing production other than through deposit insurance, it should do so directly, not by backing into another thrift debacle.

No one can accurately project the cost of implementing this program to clean up the mess. Certainly the cost should be minimized by staging the disposition of assets acquired when associations fail. Flooding real estate markets will reduce amounts received and cause inappropriate disruption. While the "repair bill" cannot be borne primarily by the surviving firms, to exculpate them will be politically impossible. If, for example, thrifts were to accept a claim on their earnings of $25 billion over the next five years, heavy though this toll would be, they could at least see the possibility of subsequently operating in a reasonably healthy environment. By appropriating the balance, $50 billion, over the same period, Congress would enjoy the same expectation. The thrift industry and the legislature would want assurances, however, that this time regulators would in fact handle the cleanup properly and not just shove problems under the rug.

In September the retiring Senate Banking Committee chairman, William Proxmire, proposed an appropriation of $20 billion to supplement industry funds, after eight years of dogged refusal by Congress to admit that it had cooperated in perpetrating a disaster. Finally the drumbeat of criticism had produced an effect. At this writing (October 1988), it appears that a new president who presents a coherent plan, appoints a competent team, and shares the political heat generated by advocating large governmental expenditures and closing hundreds of thrifts can gain congressional authority to clean up the mess and so regulate thrifts that another and even worse mess is not created in the future.

In fact, the point of debate may well shift from whether taxpayers will pay anything to whether they will pay everything. Understandably, the executives of healthy associations will insist that "the government made the mistakes and the government should bear the cost of correcting them, not those of us who ran our businesses properly." They will have a point, but they will also be beneficiaries of a program to pare down the industry so that survivors can earn decent returns on sufficient equity to protect FSLIC. Once more their franchise will have real value. They must pay their fair share to accomplish a purpose that serves not only their interests but also the public's. Both parties, however, have a right to demand from the regulators efficient management of the workout and careful oversight to prevent a recurrence. What actually happens in the next few years should be the last chapter of the thrift debacle.

Notes

1. The Golden Years and the Great Depression

1. Charles S. Tippetts, *State Banks and the Federal Reserve System* (New York: Van Nostrand, 1929), 1–2.

2. The Keynesian Miracle: 1945–1966

1. Ned Eichler, *The Merchant Builders* (Cambridge, Mass.: MIT Press, 1982).

4. Deregulation Critique and Action

1. Yair Aharoni, *The No-Risk Society* (Chatham, N. J.: Chatham House, 1981), 205.

2. Ibid.

3. Jay Janis, "Dealing with Inflation: Ideology vs. Pragmatism," in *Savings and Loan Asset Management under Deregulation*, Federal Home Loan Bank of San Francisco, Proceedings of the Sixth Annual Conference, San Francisco, California, December 8–9, 1980 (San Francisco: Federal Home Loan Bank of San Francisco, n.d.), 11–12.

4. Kenneth A. McLean, "Legislative Background of the Depository Institutions Deregulation and Monetary Control Act of 1980," in ibid., 27.

5. Thomas J. McIntyre, "A Senatorial View of Change in

the Savings and Loan Industry," in *Change in the Savings and Loan Industry*, Federal Home Loan Bank of San Francisco, Proceedings of the Second Annual Conference, San Francisco, California, December 9–10, 1976 (San Francisco: Federal Home Loan Bank of San Francisco, n.d.), 7.

6. Fred Balderston, *Thrifts in Crisis: Transformation of the Savings and Loan Industry* (Cambridge, Mass.: Ballinger, 1986), 148.

7. Edward J. Kane, "Institutional Implications of the Changing Regulatory and Technological Framework of S&L Competition," in *Change in the Savings and Loan Industry*, Federal Home Loan Bank of San Francisco, Proceedings of the Second Annual Conference, San Francisco, California, December 9–10, 1976 (San Francisco: Federal Home Loan Bank of San Francisco, n.d.), 222.

8. Ibid., 222–25.

9. Ibid., 235.

10. Ibid.

11. Anthony M. Frank, "Institutional Implications of the Changing Regulatory and Technological Framework of S&L Competition," in ibid., 246–47.

12. McLean, "Legislative Background," 21.

5. The Great Depression Revisited: 1981–1982

1. Richard T. Pratt, "Perspective of the Chairman," in *Strategic Planning for Economic and Technological Change in the Financial Services Industry*, Federal Home Loan Bank of San Francisco, Proceedings of the Eighth Annual Conference, San Francisco, California, December 9–10, 1982 (San Francisco: Federal Home Loan Bank of San Francisco, n.d.), 4.

2. Ibid., 44.

3. Ibid.

4. Ibid., 46.

5. Ibid.

6. Interview with author, December 1987.

7. Edward J. Kane, *The Gathering Crisis in Federal Deposit Insurance* (Cambridge, Mass.: MIT Press, 1985).

8. Federal Home Loan Bank Board, *Agenda for Reform* (Washington, D.C.: Federal Home Loan Bank Board, 1983), 16.

9. Ibid., 17.

10. Ibid., 39.

11. Ibid.

12. Ibid.

13. Ibid., 42.

14. Ibid., 18.

6. Disaster Strikes: 1983–1987

1. Kenneth Rosen, "The Transition Problem for the Savings and Loan Industry," in *Savings and Loan Asset Management under Deregulation*, Federal Home Loan Bank of San Francisco, Proceedings of the Sixth Annual Conference, San Francisco, California, December 8–9, 1980 (San Francisco: Federal Home Loan Bank of San Francisco, n.d.), 112.

2. Ibid., 13.

3. General Accounting Office, *Financial Audit, Federal Savings and Loan Insurance Corporation's 1986 and 1985 Financial Statements*, GAO/AFMD-87-41, May 27, 1987 (Washington, D.C.: General Accounting Office, 1987), 6–7.

4. House Committee on Government Operations, *Federal Home Loan Bank Supervision and Failure of Empire Savings and Loan Association of Mesquite, Texas*, Forty-fourth Report, August 6, 1984 (Washington, D.C.: U.S. Government Printing Office, 1984).

5. Ibid., 6.

6. Ibid., 5.

7. Ibid., 6.

8. Ibid., 50.

9. Ibid., 9.

10. House Committee on Energy and Commerce, Subcommittee on Oversight and Investigations, *Hearings*, 99th Cong., 1st sess., June 19, July 15, July 19, Sept. 11, 1985 (Serial N. 99-63), 1.

11. Ibid., 2.

12. Ibid., 257.

13. Ibid., 118.

14. Ibid., 448–49.

15. Ibid., 643.

16. Ibid., 648–49.

17. Ann Imse and Jonathan Lasner, "Saving and Looting," *Register* (Nov. 1987), 8, 9, 10, 11.

7. Assessment

1. Eichler, *The Merchant Builders*, 227–28.

2. Ibid., 278.

3. Ibid., 279.

Select Bibliography

American Council of Life Insurance. *Life Insurance Fact Book.* Washington, D.C., 1986.

Balderston, Fred. *Thrifts in Crisis.* Cambridge, Mass.: Ballinger, 1985.

Barth, James R., R. Dan Brumbaugh, and Daniel Saverhaft. *Failure Costs of Government-Regulated Financial Firms: The Case of Thrift Institutions.* Federal Home Loan Bank Board, Office of Policy and Economic Research. Research Paper no. 23. Washington, D.C.: FHLBB, 1986.

Brumbaugh, R. Dan, Jr. *Thrifts Under Siege.* Cambridge, Mass.: Ballinger, 1988.

California Savings and Loan Commissioner. *Annual Reports.* Sacramento, 1960.

Carron, Andrew S. *The Plight of Thrift Institutions.* Washington, D.C.: The Brookings Institution, 1981.

Carson, Deane, ed. *Banking and Monetary Studies.* Homewood, Ill.: R. B. Irwin, 1963.

Downs, Anthony. *The Revolution in Real Estate Finance.* Washington, D.C.: The Brookings Institution, 1985.

Eichler, Ned. *The Merchant Builders.* Cambridge, Mass.: MIT Press, 1982.

Ewalt, Josephine Hedges. *A Business Reborn.* Chicago: American Savings and Loan Institute Press, 1962.

Federal Home Loan Bank Board. *Agenda for Reform*. Washington, D.C., March 1983.
———. *Annual Reports*. Washington, D.C., 1950.
———. *Quarterly Activity Reports*. Washington, D.C., 1980.
Friedman, Milton, and Anna Jacobsen Schwartz. *A Monetary History of the United States, 1867–1960*. Princeton: Princeton University Press, 1963.
Grebler, Leo. *The Future of Thrift Institutions*. Danville, Ill.: Interstate Printers and Publishers, 1971.
Grebler, Leo, Maul David Blank, and Louis Winnick. *Capital Formation in Residential Real Estate*. Princeton: Princeton University Press, 1956.
Hughes, James W., and George Sternlieb. *The Dynamics of American Housing*. New Brunswick, N. J.: Center for Urban Policy Research, 1987.
Kane, Edward J. *The Gathering Crisis in Federal Deposit Insurance*. Cambridge, Mass.: MIT Press, 1985.
Kendall, Leon. *The Savings and Loan Business*. Englewood Cliffs, N. J.: Prentice-Hall, 1962.
Mortgage Bankers Association. *Real Estate Finance and Housing: 1987 Outlook and Fact Book*. Washington, D.C., 1987.
President's Inter-Agency Task Force on Regulation Q. *Deposit Interest Rate Ceilings and Housing Credit*. Washington, D.C.: Department of the Treasury, August 1979.
Russell, Horace. *Savings and Loan Associations*. Albany, N.Y.: M. Bender, 1960.
San Francisco Federal Home Loan Bank. *Annual Conference Proceedings*. San Francisco, 1975–1987.
United States League for Savings Associations. *Fact Books*. Chicago, 1960.
Welfing, Weldon. *Mutual Savings Banks*. Cleveland: Press of Case Western Reserve University, 1968.
White, Eugene Nelson. *The Regulation and Reform of American Banking, 1900–1929*. Princeton: Princeton University Press, 1983.

Index

Compositor: G & S Typesetters, Inc.
Text: 11/14 Aster
Display: Helvetica Condensed and Aster
Printer: Maple-Vail
Binder: Maple-Vail